Clattering Clogs

By the same author:

LANCASHIRE NICKNAMES AND SAYINGS
(Dalesman Publishing Company)

CONCERNING CLOGS
(Dalesman Publishing Company)

Clattering Clogs

"Clogiana" collected and compiled by

Bob Dobson

1981
Landy Publishing Company

ISBN: 0 9507692 0 7

Printed by Galava Printing Company Limited, Nelson, Lancashire.

Contents

On t' drawers between pot dogs

A LINK WI' T' PAST (page 16)

Introduction

Clogs are champion. I've always thought so and know I always will. I want to tell the world so, and this book is part of my plans. But there's much more to explaining why I've compiled this book. It's got to do with my love for Lancashire, her folk, her speech and the great bond between Lancashire and clogs. To me the two words are synonymous.

There has been only one book written about clogs. I wrote it. I haven't written this book, I've simply knocked it together from poems, stories and facts in my collection so that everyone can read some splendid writing about clogs, and share with me a love of this wood and leather footwear. I hope that you enjoy the book and agree with me when you've finished it that clogs are special. They have souls as well as soles.

My thanks are due to many people, without whose help, co-operation and encouragement this book would not have been published. Firstly, all the contributors for agreeing to have their work published (and for writing it in the first place). Then, in no particular order, to Barbara Blundell for designing the cover, to William Amos and his staff at "*Lancashire Life*" for allowing publication of many of the items previously published in that fine magazine, to Roy, Frank and Paul Walkely for having faith in clogs, to Bill Mitchell and David Joy of the "*Dalesman*" for releasing me from my contract so that I could pursue an ambition, to Brian Ormerod for his drawings, to my friends in the Lancashire Dialect Society and the Lancashire Authors Association for putting up with me continually mentioning clogs, and to my wife for putting up with my collecting of clogiana (no complaints about the weight of clog irons and tools in the loft).

Staining, Blackpool — July 1981

No matter where your clogs were bought,
We can them repair.
And when you think they're fit for nought,
We'll make them fit to wear.

(An advertising "jingle" c. 1900)

1. Pure Nostalgia (Silly and Sentimental)

In this part of the book I am including those poems which concern themselves with times gone by and with fond memories. Schooldays, walking in the snow with "pads" or "cloggieboggies" on, grandmas and grandads, they are all remembered:-

First of all, a grand poem by Harvey Kershaw, who was awarded the M.B.E. for his services to Lancashire and its dialect. This poem can be heard on the record "Deep Lancashire" (Topic 12T188).

CLOGS

As soon as Aw were owd enough
To toddle on mi own, deawn t' clough,
They made me wear - 'cos lone were rough ...
Some clogs.

When later-on, Aw went to skoo',
Because mi mother made mi goo,
Wi' temper, Aw punced t' noses through ...
Mi clogs!

Skoo'-maister, 'at Aw had just then,
Oft gi' mi t' stick - but more so when ...
He saw 'at Aw'd forgot to clen
Mi clogs.

Like aw young lads, Aw loved a lark,
Aw liked to make clog-irons - spark;
Aw cracked, through doin' it in t' dark ...
Mi clogs.

Mi fayther went off at deep-end,
When he feawned eawt, an' he made mi bend,
An' Aw felt what power his foot could lend ...
To clogs!

If bigger lads at top o' t' broo,
Should try to bash mi, coomin' for' t' skoo',
One thing'd allus poo mi through,
Mi clogs!

Fro' skoo' Aw went hauve-time at t'mill,
Wheer a skip for bobbins Aw'd to fill;
Mi fust week's wage, just settled t' bill ...
For new clogs.

At eighteen, Aw were cooartin' strong,
But sad to say, it didn't last long,
For hoo said, when Aw axed her what were wrong
"It's thi clogs".

That hurt so mich - Aw welly scriked,
An' after tay, to bed Aw piked,
But Aw feawnd a lass 'at said hoo liked ...
Mi clogs.

We were wed i' June o' t' followin' year,
Th' owd church were crommed - yo' couldn't stir!
That's th' only time Aw didn't wear ...
Mi clogs.

Aw'm owder neaw, bi fifty year,
Let them 'at want, ha' shoon to wear,
Aw'll be owd-fashioned, an' prefer ...
Mi clogs.

Shoon nip yo'r feet, just like a vice,
(Aw've had some - an' it's noan so nice)
If yo' han too - tak my advice ...
Try clogs!

If yo've getten a job like shiftin' sond in,
Or "bug-blindin" yo'r upsteers londin',
Yo'll need a gradely "under-stondin'" ...
Try clogs!

Two things yo'll find, browt Lancashire fame,
An' one were cotton an' t' cotton-frame,
But as for t' other - and there's nobbut one name ...
An' that's - clogs!

C.L.O.G.S. — Clogs!

Harvey was still in reminiscent mood when he wrote the following poem, "Fire-leet fancy". It can be heard on "Lancashire Sings Again" by Harvey and Mary Kershaw on Topic 12TS302.

FIRE-LEET FANCY

Sometimes, i' t' warmth o' t' fire-leet's blaze,
Aw ceawer an' dream o' bye-gone days,
An' see owd faces as Aw gaze,
Like one mon co'd Owd Yogger;
A quare nick-name, yo' mun admit,
Folk said twer noather fun, nor skit,
Whate'er th' reason were for it,
He were eawr village clogger.

Wi' t, barm-skin teed areawnd his waist,
He fashioned clogs for every taste,
Wi' straps or buckles, clasped or laced,
For which some warkers sighed;
His bench were cluttered wi' o maks,
Pinchers, an' hommers, nails an' tacks,
Awls, tachin'-end, an' hempen-flax,
An' lots o' stuff beside.

Lined up on t' shelf, for yo' to view,
Were clogs wi' uppers red, or blue,
Red-welted clogs wi'brass nails too,
A picther to behowd;
He'd clogs, thick sowled, wi capples on,
To plez e'en th' hardest warkin' mon,
An' clogs for babbies, second to none,
For keepin' eawt th' cowd.

Aw loved to watch, when-e'er Aw could,
Th' owd clogger makkin' sowls fro' wood,
Long-shaper, th' hollower, or t' gripper, stood
I' t' stocks, wi' blades 'at shone;
Wood-shavin's clustered reawnd his feet,
Made noses twitch, wi' t' smell so sweet,
If Aw should aks, Aw allus geet
Some chips, for t' fire awhom.

Clog-irons hung on rack or rail,
I' pairs, an' sizes, deawn to scale,
He'd laces, an blackin', theer, for sale,
An' tins o' dubbin', too;
In t' shop, beheend a cubbort door,

Were names an' chalk-marks, by th' score,
But what folk owed, yo' con be sure,
Nobbut th' owd clogger knew.

To ceawer on t' form in t' clogger's shop,
Each Saturday morn, childer'd hop,
They'd marlock theer, till towd to stop,
Then squabble as to who were t' next;
Th' owd clogger ceawered deawn at his bench,
His last, between his knees he'd clench,
Then brokken irons fro' t' clogs he'd wrench.
Then new irons were fixed.

Neaw t' clogger fades, as t' deein' flame
Shunts into t' fire, its warmth to claim,
Owd Yogger then, is but a name,
'at memory howds fast;
A maister o' his trade, when wick,
He knew each knack, an' every trick,
For at his job, yo' ne'er could lick
Yon craftsmon o' th' past.

One of the most oft-recalled memories of years gone by is of the sound made by clogs in the early mornings as their wearers made their way to their labours. It has been called "the iron-shod reveille", and the "Darwen artillery".

CLOG CONCERTO OF THE TWENTIES (by Malcolm Sellers)

Soft in the distance
Like Debussy,
Growing louder like Ravel,
Becoming raucous as Wagner,
The CLOGS.

Down the alleys,
Along the streets,
A rousing swelling concerto
Of clog-clad feet.

Down to the mills
At a yawn past six,
Faces pale as dinner plates,
Sepia shadows shuffling by
Beneath the shroud
Of dawning skies.

Pools of gaslight
Sad and strange,
The silhouettes of mills
Emerging, smoke meandering
To the stars
Fading behind the Pennine hills.

Clatter, clatter, clog sounds
Dying, echoes clinging
Like tumbled tambourines ...
Leather and wood
And bits or iron
Sounding through these distant dreams.

TIME SIGNALS (by Mary Burge)

I needed no transistor,
In my early working days,
No impersonal time signals
To help me on my way.

I could tell what time of day it was
From the people in the street
As they clattered by at intervals
With distinctive, clog shod feet.

Six thirty, that was Billy
With a firm and solid tread.
Clog irons rang in empty street,
Time to get out of bed.

Crisp and sharp at twenty-to,
Tom never changed his pace.
His clogs, well shod and shining,
A mirror for his face.

At quarter clanked big Eddie -
He was a heavy man.
He put his feet down firmly,
Was known as an 'Ale Can'.

Jim and Jack passed by my door,
Never varied by a yard.
I could hear their morning greeting,
'Nice day', or 'T' frost is hard'.

At five-to slithered Lizzie,
Clogs sparkling as she ran,
Half-eaten butty in her hand
And sure to miss her tram.

Heavy steps and light ones,
No two were quite the same.
As regular as clockwork.
My morning signals came.

But clogs are gone and people, too,
And nothing in their place
But soft-soled shoes and time signals
From a voice without a face.

CLOGS (by Rosamund Fishwick)

Clogs, clogs. How they clatter on the cobbled streets.
We allus 'ed to weer 'em. Mornin', noon an' neet.
T' chap who used t' mek em was a master at his job,
An' brass nails he put round t' sole - that was an extra bob.

Twelve lung hours wi stood in t'mill,
From early morn till neet.
But them owd clogs helped us
Wi eawr tired an' achin' feet.

A ha-penny stick o' blackin',
Wi spit an' polish too,
Med them clogs breet an' shiny.
Allus just like new.

Now when wi hed new cawkers on,
We med them sparks fly high.
Kickin' o'er on t'causa
When it wer nice an' dry.

Ah think we hed most fun of aw
When street wer thick wi snow.
Wi'd gret pads on eawr clogs,
Then in t' gutter they'd go.

When weather wer so very cold,
From out o't fire we'd tek
A red hot cinder, glowin' red.
It warmed em up, by heck.

That little clasp in t'middle
Were brass, an shone so breet.
Ah can't tell thi any more,
But them clogs wer grand, an just reet.

THE DAWN BRIGADE (by Peter Thornley)

At dawn I hear the tramping
Of a thousand marching clogs;
A wailing and a stamping
Of the folk in working togs.
I hear teeth go chitter-chatter,
Children's feet go pitter-patter,
And the 'cokers' clitter-clatter,
In the swirling, curling fog.

On and upwards, footsteps blending,
Over steep and cobbled hills;
Treading cold and never-ending
Paths to dark satanic mills.
Still the echo of the chatter,
Murmuring voices nitter-natter,
And the wind it doesn't matter
To these individuals.

For the mills are dead and crumbling
And the dawn brigade has gone;
But the old familiar rumbling
Of their footsteps lingers on.
If you listen in the morning,
When the cold grey day is dawning,
You may sometimes hear them yawning
As they pass you, one by one.

CLOGS (by Arthur Platt)

At half-past six in the morning,
You may hear the rhythmic beat
Of clogs, that are rattle-attle-attling,
Along the drowsy village street:
To her work, in the mill, the factory-lass
Trips daintily, and neat,
And the merriest sound in Lancashire
Is the music from her feet.

Chorus-

Clogs! clogs! clogs with neatly pointed toes,
Little brass nails are studded round;
The soles are wooden, iron bound;
And the lasses go, with heel and toe,
Rat, tat, tat, on the cobbled ground.

Shoes are made from Crocodile skins,
With heels which higher grow;
Patent leather's not for wintry weather,
Nor Suede for slush and snow;
But a lass's clogs, which she buckles on
Are the 'cutest' things you know;
Her feet are shod like peas in a pod,
They're gradely snug; heigho!

Chorus-

It's ill when Mills are closing down,
For all the hands must leave;
If India and China did not buy
Bland books and silent engines grieve;
Workless folk must draw the dole,
From famine there's no reprieve,
And the music of the clogs is still'd
When ther's nought to spin and naught to weave.

Chorus -

Clogs! clogs! clogs! with neatly pointed toes,
Little brass nails are studded round,
The soles are wooden, iron-bound,
But, with times so hard, they no longer sound,
Rat, tat, tat, on the cobbled ground.

Most of the clog-poems I have collected are of recent origin, as most of the writers of yesteryear neglected the subject. I have been fortunate to have had poems written specially for me, and to have been in the happy position of being a judge in dialect writing competitions when good poems and stories have been submitted. You'll be seeing them in this book. One whose heart was in the right place was John Thomas Baron (Jack o'Ann's - 1856-1922), a Blackburn poet of the highest ranking.

JOHNNY'S CLOGS

Howd on, theer! Dunnot use 'em rough, but put 'em gently deawn;
They're nobbut hawf-worn clogs to yo, wi' tops o' musty breawn;
To me, they're sacred links 'at bind my thowts to one i' th' mowd;
Eawr Johnny wore those clogs afooar Deeath med him stiff an' cowd.

They're but a pair o' little clogs, wi' irons rusty red,
Yet thowts they wakken i' my heart, ov a life-star 'at's fled.
For th' gloom o' grief seems darker neaw, an' Life's nowt near as sweet
As when he used to welcome me wi' hooam smiles every neet.

Tho' th' sod's bin o'er him mony a while, to life he's gi'en a grace;
Oft reawnd my cot aw wond'ring stare - there's summat eawt o' place.
That lad wur th' best mate 'at aw hed i' sunshine or i' storm.
Wur aw a King, my creawn aw'd give, to clap th' familiar form.

No other eye could shine like his; his speech, so soft an' mild,
Fell o' my ears like music-strains, - he wur my darling child.
No hand seemed hawf so nice to grip, nor greetin' e'er so kind
As his; an' neaw aw seem to hear his voyce i' every wind.

Last neet, aw see a little star, 'at fairly pleased my eye,
It seemed o ov a flutter theer, heigh up i' th' dusky sky.
An' then a thowt flashed thro' my mind 'at med my eyeseet dim.
He wur my child! aw stood on th' earth, an' looked tort Heaven, on him.

Con he be waitin' for me theer, hawf-way fro' th' gowden Throne?
Wur them his wings 'at fluttered breet heigh i' thoose realms unknown?
His bonny face seems allus near, an' th' love for him shall be
Held sacred i' this heart o' mine reight to Eternity.

I think the same muse who visited Jack o' Ann's also inspired Harvey Kershaw to write:

A LINK WI' T' PAST

Among owd things Aw prize awhom,
There's a pair o' babby's clogs,
Mi mother used tu show 'em off
On t' drawers, between pot dogs.

Th' uppers are polished spick an' span,
An' th' irons look welly new,
There's brass nails reawnd t' red leather welts,
An' a shinin' buckle, too.

Aw sometimes think o' t' babby's feet,
'at those clogs helped tu cover,
An', in imagination, yer
That childt skrike for its mother.

As soon as t' childt had larned tu stond,
An' toddle reawnd t' mother's knee,
They bowt it little clogs tu wear,
Like th' rest o' th' family.

Its tiny feet were seldom still,
But allus busy trottin',
They pattered gaily reawnd th' floor
Forever mischief spottin'.

That childt is neaw a full grown mon,
Wi' childer of his own
An' oftimes when th' owl-leet has coom,
Wi' pride yon clogs are shown.

Who were th' childt 'at wore th' clogs?
Yo'r axin' neaw, maybe,
It's a mon yo' should know middlin' weel,
For, bless yo'r life, twer ME.

Norah Collier, a St Annes lady, sent me the following poem after reading my book "Concerning Clogs", and told me how many memories I had evoked for her. I hope that I've done the same for others too, and given some pleasure into the bargain.

CONCERNING CLOGS

Eeh lad, tha's taen mi back
Ay, more na sixty years.
Tha's med mi laugh, tha's taught mi lots,
An Ah shed a couple o' tears.

Oh ay, Ah sparked mi clogs
Most times at Ah wor eawt,
But nivver when mi Mam wor theer,
Or Ah'd a getten misen a cleawt.

When Ah think o' t' pads Ah med,
Walkin' tall in t' snow.
An' me allus bein' a little 'un,
It felt reight good yo' know.

When Ah wer comin' hooam frae t' schoo',
Cowd weather didna matter.
An if Ah needed irons on,
Mi mam ud sooak t' clog i' watter.

She didna want t' soles crackin'
When t' clogger banged t' nails in.
Even coppers meant a lot to her,
Wi no big wage comin' in.

Ah wore mi clogs to t' factory
Long after Ah wer wed.
Mi feet ud still be warm enough
As warm as when i' bed.

When Ah wer a little kid,
Ah could laike i' country bogs,
Knowin' Ah wouldn't get witcherd
In mi wood an' leather clogs.

But Ah didn't care fer cleanin, em,
Cos them days we used blackin',
An, a bit of spit if it was hard,
Cherry Blossom polish wer lackin'.

But when Ah geet a bit more pride,
Ah cleaned mi clogs each neet.
Ah welly could see mi face in 'em,
They really were a treat.

Ah'd don mi special cleanin' pinny,
One med frae sugar sacks,
An' rubbed 'em wi a tooth brush 'andle
An' a piece o' cobbler's wax.

Oh ay - You've oppened up t' flood gates,
An' Ah wish Ah hed mi clogs still.
But Ah'll tell yo this - When Ah hed 'em,
They wer t' cleanest clogs i' t' mill.

An' Edwin Waugh - Ah know his works.
"Ned Waff" - as Lankies say.
Ah send 'is message back to you,
That goes fer ivvery day.

Good poetry isn't simply rhyming verse, it is the setting down of thoughts from the heart. Nostalgic poems often have this quality. Sense it in Eric Holt's poem about a real owd Lancashire chap - his grandad. By the way, "clugs" is how they say "clogs" in the Bolton-Wigan-Leigh area.

GRANDAD'S CLUGS

Mi grandad's clugs sheign breet as glass
Through years o' spit an' blackin'.
'Ee's polished ev'ry nail o' brass,
Tho' t' tops er aw but crackin'.

'Ee wears 'is clugs i' rain an' drought,
Through fair an' stormy weather.
Five bob they cost him when fust bowt,
'Ond sewn, wi' 'oles in t' leather.

Them clugs 'ave rattled monny shins,
Fer grandad fancied sparrin'.
Th' owd lad were nimble on his pins,
An' t' clugs were made fer parrin'.

But grandad's parrin' days are gone,
Th' owd rockin' cheers a-pooin'.
An' t' clugs, like 'im are aw but done,
An' t' weltin's started gooin'.

But when 'ee's slipped through t' Golden Gate,
An' breathed 'is last so sweetly
'Is clugs'll slumber up bi' t' grate,
Brass nails still sheignin' breetly!

Jimmy Fell has the knack of finding just the right things to say to touch Lancashire folks' senses - humour, pathos, pride. The following two poems tell you just what I mean:-

AH'M EIGHTY-TWO - TEK A LOOK AT THE FEET

Ah'm just eighty two - tek a look at them feet,
They're good as on t' day Ah wor born,
Tek 'eed o' them toes, as straight as a die,
Tha'll noan see a sign of a corn.

Ond dosta know why? Ah'll tell thee, owd lad,
Ah've niver worn owt else but clogs,
Ah've worn 'em t' mill, Ah've worn 'em at play,
In t' fact'ry ond laikin' wi' t' dogs.

Ah've worn 'em down t' cut, Ah've worn 'em on th' 'ills,
Ah've bin ower th' ankles i' mud,
Ah've worn 'em when ticklin' fer trout down in t' beck,
Ah've worn em i' 'ail, snow ond flood.

Th' owd woman played 'ell when Ah showed up i' clogs
At church, on t' day we wor wed,
"Eeh! Thee ond thi clogs!", hoo sed, proper grim,
"Bah gum, tha'll noan wheer 'em i' bed!"

Ah've getten no time fer them posh fancy shoon
As sum sticks on th' end o' their legs,
No wonder they waddles around like owd ducks,
'Alf crippled wi' bunyons ond segs.

So just thee tek 'eed of a fella what knows,
Who's worn 'em through watter ond bogs,
Tha'll be wick as a snig, tha'll dance like a lord,
If the niver wheers owt else but clogs!

T' RING O' CLOGS

What ses Lancasheer to thee?
Is it Blackpoo' by the sea?
Is it wet ond muggy days,
Ships on 't Mersey through the 'aze,
Blackpuddings on a plate in't shops,
Industry as niver stops,
Is it shawls or whippet dogs,
Or is it just the ring o' clogs.

Tha maybe thinks o' Pendle 'ill,
Or weivers torning out fray t' mill,
'Appen t' Rovers or North End,
Weekend when tha's brass to spend.
It's 'appen t' pits ond slag 'eaps grey,
Shrimps ond Southport, Morecambe Bay,
Or gorse, ond millstone grit ond bogs,
It brings 'em back does t' ring o' clogs!

Th' owd windmill tall on Lytham Green,
Fact'ries and th'ouses in between,

Clanging trams and cobbled streets,
T' Market lit wi' flares at neets,
Gracie when hoo's singing "Salley",
Rivington, or t' Ribble Valley,
Mill lodges thick wi' newts ond frogs,
Mem'ries flood back wi't ring o' clogs!

Brass bands on Sunda' into t' park,
Cooartin' in t' lamp leet efter dark,
Treats on Knucknowles, Whit processions,
"Lakin", "Witchert", owd expressions,
These mem'ries rise up sharp ond clear,
When the sound o' clogs Ah 'ear,
It sweps away the mist ond fogs
Fray memory, does t' ring o' clogs!

Retired schoolmaster, William McDowell recalls a story of schoolboy fun:-

A PAIR OF WHITEWASHED CLOGS.

A one-time headmaster of Leigh National School, R.M. Gornall (1885 - 1919) was an ex-Army man who marched his pupils to Church in military style, his rolled umbrella over his shoulder, serving as a rifle. Clog inspection was carried out in parade ground fashion, backs as well as fronts being closely scrutinised. One poor lad, with clogs as clean as spit and brushing could achieve, was ordered to appear the following morning with the footwear blacked and polished. Then, to the tittering of his toadies, the beetle-browed head thundered "OR ELSE, WHITEWASH 'EM!"

"So that's what ol' Gornall wants, is it? Tomorrow we'll both go to schoo. There's enoof whitewash left o'er from t' petty." Harry duly stood in line with his sympathetic class-mates, the wiry little widow standing at the gate, broom over her shoulder in irreverent, deflating mimicry. "That's what yo' wanted, mester" she shouted. "Lad leaves 'ere on Friday." And leave Harry did, for the kindlier atmosphere of the British School.

A few more poems written in reminiscent mood:-

CLOGS (by Jimmy Jones)

Mary Jane, un me yo know, bin courtin' twenty yer,
Deauwn th' owd lanes walked arm i' arm, keaw's at us ud stare,
Oo sed one neet, "It's time tha knows, t' bey a double bed",
"Road things are in t' money line, ah'll, bey thi clogs instead,"
Ger a pair o' clogs owd wench, comfort tha will feel,
Allus keep two irons i' front, two moor fast on th' heel.

Once ah stood on t' city street, fine lady did approach,
"Cum wi' me young mon" oo said, whistl't fer a coach,
"Sorry luv", an shook mi yed, patted her nice dog,
Soles are deauwn t' weltin', look at mi reet clog,
Ah need a pair o' clogs owd wench, so comfort ah con feel,
It pays thi keep two irons i' front, two moor fast on th' heel.

Went to a reacehorse meetin', by gum it wur a lark,
Fro our owd pub i' charabang, seet off t' Haydock Park,
Th' only one pur on mi clogs, th' outlook seemed fer storm,
Cum whoam skint, bar th' odd two bob, mi feet wur drey an' warm,
Tha needs a pair o' clogs owd wench, so comfort tha con feel,
Allus keep two irons i' front, two moor fast on th' heel.

Religious folk cum canvassin', knocked o' my front door,
'Adachat o'er this an' that, ah've seen um aw afoor.
Towd me just hey bad ah wur, lived a life o' sin,
Met get reauwnd to joinin' um when clogs let watter in.
Thee get a pair o' clogs owd wench, comfort tha will feel,
Allus keep two irons i' front, two moor fast on th' heel.

Ther'll cum a time ah'st tak me place, ridin' in t' fust coach,
Lond up theer i' gradely style, St. Peter will approach,
"Con ah cum in", ah'll say to 'im, "Con ah walk with God?"
"Welcome, welcome" 'e 'll reply, "E likes a mon well shod".
So tak a pair o' clogs owd wench, comfort tha will feel,
Mak sure tha's geet two irons i' front, two moor fast on th' heel.

MI DAD'S BEST CLOGS (by Wilf Hill)

Brown thi' were, wi studs o' brass
hi loved them clogs mi Dad did,
better na tha loves em
and better na thi' kid.

Mi mam went on about his clogs
whenere hi shewed his face
then he'd stick em up on't mantelshlf
An' gi'em pride o' place
He loved them clogs mi Dad.

He used to go clog dancin
it helped his means test out
he were well known o round Ashton.
he'd bi famous for his dancin
or so mi father thowt.

Every neet he'd practice
click and clack and punce
wha' ever else he cudna do
at this hi were no dunce.

Charlie Chaplin came to Ashton
wi' auditions go ont stage
an ah dunna 'ave to tell ya
clog dancin were all t' rage.

Friday neet were his neet
dressed in his best togs
he went across to t' cupboard
were he alus kept his clogs
and they were gone!

Were's mi bloody clogs gone?
stuff flew all over t' place
ah thowt he'd 'ave an 'art attack
from t' colour on his face.

Mi Mam came in, from t' kitchen
"Ah dunna like tellin' thi' Jack
one of 'em fell off t' mantelshelf
an ah cudna ger it back".

"Tha cudna ger it back", he yelled,
"Tha cudna ger it back!"
The he gathered ow his bits a' things
an stuck 'em in a sack.

Mi Mam just stood there speechless
she thowt her end were nigh
as he slammed the door behind him
she just let out one cry.

We never saw mi Dad again
We never more burnt logs
and if yer should come visitin'—
for God's sake don't say 'clogs!'

Wilf's dad danced with the "Lancashire Lads", as did Charlie Chaplin.

PRIDE O' LANKYSHIRE (by Sheila Jardine)

Fer dry feet, an' waarm feet, yud find it reet hard t' beat
Th' owd clogs as wur worn, ('fore today's kids wur born.)
On t' grey cobbled streets, cum t' clatter o' feet,
Clip-cloppin', clip-cloppin', (like hosses, a-trottin'.)
Each time they touched t' ground, 't wur a real gradely *sound,*
An' sparks flew, when t' irons struck sharply, on t' stoans!
When t' Knocker-up cum, ('fore furst shift, at t' Mill,)
'is clogs used ta echo,... all t' way down ower hill;
(I' mi mind, I goes back - an' I'm sure 'earin' 'em still.)
I never was one fer yer posh, fancy togs,
They suited mi fine, *- did mi Lankyshire clogs;*
Med o' leather, *not plastic, (ta let in sum air,)*
I swaggered round Town, in mi very furst pair!
They cum i' fashion, a few years ago,
But wurn't 'alf a patch on th' owd 'uns ya know!
These wur red uns - an' blue uns, wi' flowers *painted on,*
An' t' price *they wur askin' - I'm telling ya mon*
'ud 'ave kept all *ower tribe, fer a week - mebbe two,*
Fer we'd but bread an' drippin', when pay-day wur due.
Mi dad looked just reet, *in 'is clogs, an' flat cap,*
No la-de-da nonsense - a down-to Earth chap;
An' t' Southerners sed as we all looked sa queer,
But it ne'er worried us - up i' North Lankyshire!
Now I've getten sum boots, folks still *aren't satisfied,*
"Why don't you wear shoes? Don't you have any *pride?"*
But I pays no 'eed, (as I sed ta mi wife,)
I've great 'eaps o' pride *- 'bowt th' owd Lankyshire life!!*

A LITTUL PUR O' CLOGS (by Mavis Homewood)

Ah ad no roots, Ah'd travellt fur, t' money cem an went;
As fast as Ah cud mek a bob, t' faster wor it spent.
Ah'd bet on every bloomin race, on th'orses an on't dogs,
Till wun day Ah wor browt up short bi' a littul pur o' clogs.

Thi sat theer lone an dusty, deawn in't cobbler's shop,
An suddenly mi feet grew wings, fer nothin cud ah stop;
A rusty bell clanged loudly as Ah pusht ajar yon door,
An' Ah saw th' ancient cobbler, kneelin' theer on't floor.

'e lookt at me in sum surprise so great ad bin mi 'aste;
But sumthin seemed to tell me I ad no time fer't waste.
Ah ast 'im 'ow much was them clogs as ah wor pointin' too,
'e sed te me "tha's cum in time, there aint no charge to you."

'is wurds some'ow wor not so strange, Ah took clogs in me 'and
An' knew Ah 'ad to cum back 'ome to this mi native land.
Ah cowt a plane an' fretted much fer all o't yeers ah'd wasted,
Ah wor no better off Ah knew fer 'ectic lahfe Ah'd tasted.

Mem'ries fro mi child'oot days began fer't fill mi brain,
An' Ah decided then an thur Ah'd start mi life agen.
Fer neaw Ah meant fer't settle deawn, Ah'd sell mi fancy togs,
An' Ah thankt th' Lord as 'ow Ah'd sin that littul pur o' clogs.

DYED IN THE BLACK (by Reg Palmer)

Well 'ere wi are, just thee an' me,
A pair o' 'as-bins now,
But both on us, un 'ad some fun
An' nere once 'ad a row.

Ah remember first time wi wer shod
Thi an tu fit just reat,
Does theigh remember t' fuss thi med
Afore wi went ont street.

An when wi did gu out that day
O polished up reight grand,
What wer it that thi said to us?
Nu 'punsin' now, that's banned.

But that wer tin cans, that thi meant
Not foot-bo, played ont tip,
Win scored our team a lot of goals,
These 'cappels' med um zip.

An later when t' snow covered streets
Ad turned to slush int neet,
Wi knew wid earn us keep next day
When keepin dreigh ther feet.

But that's goin back a reight long time
An things 'ave changed sin then
Folk an nu time fer us owd lass
Thil noaw turn back agen.

Ote factry steps 'ave long sin gone
An't tips no longer theer,
An if thi started clog dansin
Young uns ud think um queer.

Su 'ere wi are pushed out o' seat
Thil cob us out o'reat
A dunna think thil beat us tho
Fer keepin warm ther feet.

David Lavisher, recalls his childhood in this poem, and though he doesn't know it, he tells us he's an Owdhamer by including the word "slippy-kerry" (sometimes "slippy curry") which is old Norse meaning a slide on ice. It seems to have survived only in Oldham but not elsewhere in Lancashire.

AS AH REMEMBER CLOGS

Ah wer browt up in a cotton town,
Cloaked in smoke an' smog.
Wi'd cobbled streets an' gas lamps,
Bonnets, shawls,
An't clog.

A reg'lar kind of footwear,
This last, as must be said,
Wore by names like 'Arry,
Sid, an' Bert, an' Fred.

Early morn yu'd 'ear em,
Clankin' thru't back streets.
Way mi mother towd it,
Thi all 'ad perfect feet.
"Clogs er best fert feet," she'd say,
As shi polished mine fer school,
Some a't kids 'ad boots t'at feet,
But a din't feel a fool.

Thi used ta seem reight warm t'at feet,
Despite ther wooden bottoms.
An't leather tops, though stiff wen new,
Din't need two pair a stockins.
Wer't best a't year, wer't Winter.
Walkin 't school in't snow,
It used ta stick t'at th' irons,
Called 'Cloggy-bogs', yuh know.

Though iv yu'd walked on a slippy-kerry,
An' 'adn't realized,
Them kids, as made ther slide on t' brew,
Yuh from the floor, despised.

Wen wi played us football,
Wi allus seemed ta win.
Many a time av kicked at ball,
An' missed,
An' kicked ther shin.

Thi wern't seen much ont' dance floor,
Trippin t' light fantastic.
Yer feet wun't go
Wer yuh wanted em to,
An' yer legs ud a t'bi 'lastic.

Thi wern't reight good fer climbin,
Walls, er apple trees.
Er runnin, from yer father,
Utterin frantic pleas.

Sum ad rubber irons,
As wer quiet, an didn't slip.
Yuh could sneak up on that cheeky kid,
As last week, give 'is lip.

Thi wer ordinary folk as 'ad 'em.
Miners, an farmers, too.
An t' women in t' mills used wear 'em,
Thi were lower,
'Bout size of a shoe.
An 'ow about Morris Dancers,
Still usin 'em today,
Clogs uv bin wi us a year er two now,
A reckon ther 'ere ta stay.

Many of the people I have spoken to remember their childhood clogs, but Margaret Helliwell remembers her very first pair:

MI FUST NEW CLUGS

When aw wer jist a nipper mi muther ses to me,
"Thi grondad's cummin at Sathurdi wi a present jist fer thee."
Awst a bin wol nearly three aw guess, aw adn't gon tut schooil,
An aw cudn't play art bi missel, aw'd to sit in't yard on't stooil.

Well, Sathurdi coom an fotched mi gran an grondad off t' bus,
Thi'd a twoathri parcels i' ther hond at aw knew ud bi for us.
Aw oppened mine wi awl gret speed, to see jist wot ther wor,
An a luvly little pair o' clugs wer liggin theer on't floo-er.

Aw were sum an praad on' yon new clugs, aw put em on mi feet,
An aw tuk mi gron an grondad's hond an toddled off daan't street.
Aw clathered up an daan in't yard, an med a dreadful noise.
To show heaw mi clugs med sparks on't greawnd tut other girls an boys.

Thi were little pointed toed uns wi cutouts allso neat.
Braun calf wi real brass studs on, an straps across mi feet.
Mi mam said Clogs wer't best things made fer keeping thi feet warm,
Well, aw know aw allus wore um an it nee'r did me ne harm.

An wen awd past fer Grammar Schooil, it weren't 'ony thing aw lacked,
Aw cudn't weer mi clugs tut schooil, aw'd to wait til aw geet back,
Tugoo an put mi clugs on, speshully t' winter neets
Th'ony time at aw wer warm wer wen mi clugs wer on mi feet.

It's a pity thin gon awt o' style, thi dooant weer em ony moore,
'Sept maybe sum ut owd un's fer swillin awt ut dooar.
Altho aw've sin sum bether days sinaw geet mi clugs at t' start,
Memory o' mi fust new clugs ull stay clooase to mi heart.

A lass who worked most of her life in the shoe and slipper trade up the Rossendale Valley, Gertie Newman penned her clog-thoughts in this way:-

MI CLOGS

I used to catch t' tram
And go to mi wark,
Set off in t' dayleet
And come back in t' dark.

I went clatterin' deawn t' rooad
An' folk knew to shift,
When they yerd these gret clogs
They acted so swift.

There were good pals to me
In all sorts o' weather,
Not these fancy stilettos,
In all sorts o' leather.

One day I'd a brainwave,
I geet a fresh job,
A grand pair o' shoes
At just thirty bob.

I'd to put these owd clogs
Once more owt o' seet,
Mi boss were allus
Interested in t' feet.

I give him a black look
When he turned his back,
If he'd a just catched me
I'd a sure getten t' sack.

This new job Ah geet
Were in a grand heawse
They had a gret cat
Ut wouldn't catch a meawse.

Wherever I went,
I were allus in t' news,
All they could talk about
Were these mi new shoes.

An' so that's th' end,
O' mi faithful owd clogs,
If it weren't for t' new shoes
They'd a sent mi to t' dogs.

The title of Mary Jane Findon's poem tells us how she feels about her clogs:-

BELOVED CLOGS

Ah loved mi clogs wen ah wer young,
Mi Dad, e cleaned um all fer us;
E lined um up on t' Sunday neet;
Even t' brass nails shined reet breet.

Propper irons ah liked best, (not leather uns, thi wur a pest,)
To slide on t' Slippy Currys on t' pavements,
Tho monys-a-time we cum a cropper,
Un slipped on t' th' arse on spying t' copper.

Ah liked sparks like flints us cum from t' friction
Wen strikin t' th' irons on t' flags;
Un t' cloggy boggys wi med in t' snow;
Six inches high thi ranked.

But best of all thi wer reet warm;
Un kept mi feet warm in a storm;
So Lancashire, ahm proud to be,
Part of a legend based on thee.

Harold Lord, now living away from his native Rochdale, has committed all his clog-thoughts and memories to paper (I'm happy to say).

MEMORIES OF ROCHDALE

From a tender age I had known that clog wearers fell into class conscious groups. Some people had clogs which fastened with clumsy clips, others had trim little straps and buckles or buttons. Very posh ones had laces. Smart young ladies had dainty lightweight clogs, other females might very well wear articles that were not easily distinguishable from masculine versions. Clogs could be supplied handmade to measure for affluent people. These were likely to have prettily tooled patterns and be fitted with brass eyelets and have rows of swanky round headed brass nails, not to mention beautifully burnished and trimmed metal toe caps. Oh yes, status could be indicated by the clogs. The term 'Clever Clogs' was much in vogue and could be complimentary or derogatory, all according to the inflection of the voice.

I rather enjoyed wearing clogs and so did the other boys. It was fun. By skillfully striking the pavement at the correct angle we could cause a lovely stream of sparks to appear. The sight of a dozen small boys running at full pelt and all sparking at the toes and heels would have looked splendid on colour television.

We used to paddle in the millstream wearing our clogs, but without our socks on, we were thereby immune from sharp stones and broken glass. If we felt brave enough to risk cut feet we could always have enormous sport by sailing our clogs like little boats. This entrancing pastime could end in a calamity if a strong current swept a clog over the weir so that it was lost forever. Some poor, miserable little fellow then had to make a sad journey home and face the certainty of a thrashing. This capering in the water always produced a temporary shrinkage of the leather and I well remember having uncomfortable feet for about 15 minutes on the way home until my clogs recovered.

Kicking with clogs was known as 'punsing' and the clogged foot was a brutal weapon. The days of commercialised clog fights which did not end until a contestant fell unconscious had happily vanished long before my time. Would you believe that on one occasion as a penalty for some misdemeanor at home, I was shoved down the cellar steps and locked in. But I had my clogs on and I began to punse the door. It was badly cracked, in next to no time I was released and it was never tried again.

Clog dancing was a thing I liked to watch, but performers gradually became rare and the art seemed to disappear. In winter frozen ponds were a source of delight, we could slide beautifully on our clog irons and we never tired of it. Icy pavements formed a real hazard to elderly people and serious falls were quite frequent. Incidentally there seemed to be more snow around in those days and the result of snowfalls was quite interesting. Snow produced cloggibogs. Cloggibogs! What on earth are cloggibogs do you ask? I'll tell you. It was like this, walking on snow trapped a thin layer between the clog irons and compressed it into ice, the further one walked the thicker that layer became, and one became taller and taller as a cloggibog formed on each foot. Cloggibogs were platform soles with a vengeance. The maximum height was about 2½ inches and at this stage they were usually so heavy that they suddenly fell off on the pavement looking like delicately moulded blocks of ice. It was considered good manners to stop and kick one's cloggibogs into the gutter leaving the pavement free from obstruction. All cloggibogs were solemnly kicked off at the journey's end. It was always possible to deduce who had already arrived home from a study of the deposited cloggibogs.

I ought to say that cloggibogs could be perverse, one might build up to a greater height than the other and walking would then become very awkward. Sometimes one cloggibog would prematurely detach itself whilst the other would stick on and defy all efforts to kick it off. A poor young lass could find herself seriously handicapped, especially if she were struggling with her shawl in the icy wind at the same time. She might have to rely on the chivalry of a passer by. From such a fortuitous encounter romance had been known to blossom. Spiteful tongues hinted that some such incidents were deliberately planned and it had been obvious from the very start that the brazen young so and so had never, never, really had cloggibog trouble at all. Ah well—Bonny lasses have always had to use their wits. Those girls had no make up, no false eye lashes, no expensive hair dos. Nothing much more than a shawl, a pair of dainty clogs and a very genuine accent.

The clatter of clogs was never heard on Sundays. Churches, Chapels and Sunday schools were all well attended but I feel that there would have been many more devout Christians but for an embargo on Sabbath clog wearing. There was an unwritten rigid code that those who could not obtain shoes for Sunday wear, just stayed indoors. It was accepted that when our Lord Jesus Christ said "Suffer the little children to come unto me and forbid them not" He meant unless they were wearing clogs.

Children began with clogs at about the age of three. Clogs were comfortable and durable. It was known that the clog irons would gradually wear out, but a visit to the cloggers shop soon put that right at a very small cost. Clog irons were nailed on with special clog nails and the process resembled horse shoeing except that no heating was needed. Repairs were usually on a 'While you wait' basis because very few had an alternative footwear. It was folly to neglect the renewal of clog irons as this soon resulted in a cracked clog sole and new clog soles were expensive.

One day, after the Angels had descended to take away yet another of my little playmates, I was instructed to go along and take my last look at his earthly frame. I hurried to the big house at the corner, knocked, and was soon ushered into the best front room. There, resembling a waxen doll, lay his mortal remains. I gazed intently, content in my belief that he was happily looking down at me from on high, until I suddenly realised that he would be aware of my dreadful breach of etiquette, that he would be staring at my footwear. I had entered their best front room wearing my clogs. I burst into tears. "I forgot to take my clogs off before I came in" I sobbed to his young mother. "Never thee mind" she said. To my intense surprise, she then passed her fingers through my hair.

Times changed and progress of a sort made rapid headway. Almost overnight it seemed, clogs and the cloggers shops vanished. Clogs not only became unfashionable, they became unmentionable. Nobody admitted having any knowledge thereof, not even when they had been handmade. The entire subject was rated as being extremely low. Clogs were now destined to be held in contempt and derision. A symbol of subjection associated with a simple and humble type of people with rather questionable backgrounds. The world famous early morning clatter disappeared from the streets of Lancashire and no one ever thought to record it on wax or tape.

(See also Harold's article "*Clog Consciousness*" in *Lancashire Life* December 1978).

This photograph of two lads (John Tomlinson, on the left, and his mate called Shepherd) was taken in 1903 at Haslingden. Photograph loaned by the Helmshore Local History Society. What stories those clogs could tell.

Suzanne Lawless won this handsome belt for her skill in dancing the Lancashire hornpipe at the Saddleworth Folk Festival 1980. The competitors dance on an old mounting-block outside a church after helping to pull a rushcart decorated in traditional style. The Festival is held each August Bank Holiday weekend.

Above: The belt for the Lancashire & Cheshire Clogdancing Champion specially made for the Fylde Folk Festival by Don MacFarlane, craftsman in leather, of Jedburgh. Photo kindly loaned by Sue Bousefield.

Below: A pair of clogs made to fit in a matchbox by Jack Murray, an old Accrington clogger, alongside a 100 years old pair made for a child. It is interesting to note how children's feet have become bigger since wholesome food and welfare services became available. The clogs are soled with a strip of leather to give extra wear.

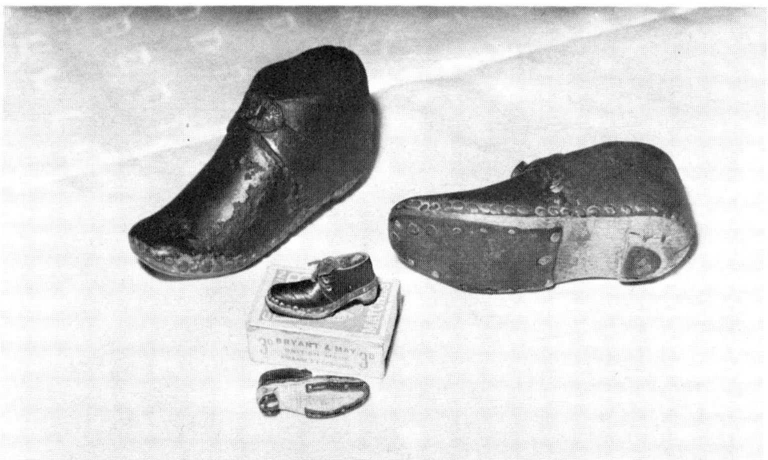

Above: A scene from a 1950 film "Lancashire Pride" showing Colne clogdancer James Starkie. Photo kindly loaned by Geoff Crambie.

Below: Block-makers at work about 1905 at Claughton. Photo kindly loaned by Reuben Truswell (Clarkson's Cloggers).

2. Cloggers and Clog Shops

Many of the people I have spoken to about their clog-wearing days have told me of the great pleasure they had (and I shared this) in sitting on the wooden form that was in most clog-shops, waiting bare-foot for their clogs to be fettled by the clogger. He was always an old man, though of course that was only in the eyes of kids.

In byegone days, a lot of lads who were disabled in some way were trained to become cloggers and shoe repairers. The asylums and poor-houses employed people to train youngsters in these crafts. Some deaf and dumb lads were trained in this way. One of them later bought himself a shop in Baxenden ("Bash" to locals) near Accrington. Jack Walmsley was known to all quite simply as "Jackie Dummy". His lad later took over the shop but right up to him retiring in 1981, locals persisted in referring to the shop as "Jackie Dummy's". To enter that shop was to step back in time. The dust of years was everywhere, as was the smell of wood and leather. Nothing had ever been tidied up. A calendar hung on the wall—it was 1941 there right to the very end, and you could quickly tell when t'Stanley were playing next in the Third Division North. Marvellous. Jack Walmesley (Junior) was blessed with a wonderful memory, as most cobblers are. Les Bond recalls that one day he was passing the shop and remembered that he had taken some shoes in for mending some three years before and hadn't collected them. Getting inside, Les explained he had left the shoes "some months back" and apologised for not calling sooner. Jack said he remembered them, soon found them amongst the piles he had, apologised for being busy and said, "They'll be ready on Friday". Former "Basher", Irene Hargreaves recalls her early days in the shop:-

JACKIE DUMMY

The old clogger I knew as a child has long since passed on, but the shop is exactly the same now, except his son who now owns it can speak. I feel now it was terrible to refer to the old man as everybody did because he was deaf and dumb, as was his wife. As I look back on the tricks we used to play on him I feel quite guilty. He had a wooden tray with deep holes in, each one filled with different nails and we used to mix them all up. He used to sit facing the window, which hardly allowed any light as it was full of cardboard adverts, shoes etc. and behind him was a sewing machine which we used to try and play with, but immediately you touched it, he would turn round and shake his fist and mutter and growl, which always terrified me. He was a small man with moustache and really very gentle and he had a form on the side of one wall and when we made far too much racket, rocking it about, his wife would appear. She was very tall and straight as a rod and without so much as a sound, just her stance made us behave immediately. I realize now it was the front room of their house. He had hung about groups of irons, "heels" and "fronts" and "sets" and at school we would arrange to have a heel iron replaced if one had a crush on any particular person and many a perfectly good iron 'came off' at play times as an excuse. As the chip shop was and still is next door, we would buy our 'chips', eat them on the form and were always willing to let anybody go before us, to prolong our stay. The way he made a clog sole from a flat piece of wood and fastened the leather round it with brass nails always intrigued me. My own clogs were ankle straps and how I hated them. My brother's were much heavier, laced like a shoe and had 'toe caps' on. My father worked in a dye house and he had 'lace up' clogs. I can smell the leather now and when taken from a very hot foot, must have been awful for him I'm sure as he put it on the last. My Mother died when I was young and I thought 'Hurrah no more clogs for me in the mill' so off I went very posh in my shoes. Come 3 p.m. I could hardly walk about the 'alley', so I left my clogs at work and used shoes to and from work.

They used to say it encouraged a child to walk quicker, hearing the sound of the iron, but the reason one lad wore them was because his grandmother was blind and she could hear where he was in the house and back street. I can see how the clogger re-ironed the clog. He ripped off the broken iron as it had usually worn thin. It always reminded me of the dentist with teeth as he ripped out old nails, then in previous nail holes he put a small peg of wood and hammered that, then the nail and hammered that. If a clog sole was cracked he would shake his head and point to the crack or write on his slate with pencil. It screeched and made my teeth feel awful. The things we wrote on that slate was nobody's business and some even did their homework on it. Yes that shop will always be known for ever by true "Bashers" as Jackie Dummys, when we know full well now it is Jackie Walmesleys.

Bert Williams, living in Canada with his heart in Bolton, remembers much the same:

THE CLOGGERS

The front parlour window had been replaced with a large shop front and what was formerly the parlour was lined with shelves and fitted with counters. The small back room, which used to be the kitchen, was now used as the clog repairing shop and here four skilled workmen were kept fully employed, making and repairing clogs.

The workmen sat around a low built work bench, the top of which was divided into small sections which held broad-headed nails, tiny wooden plugs, clog irons of various sizes and narrow strips of leather. On one corner of the bench was a heavily forged steel loop, in which the clogger hooked his heavy, razor-sharp cutting tool when shaping the wooden soles from pieces of alder.

Upto the early 1920's, clogs were the most popular kind of footwear of the working people of Bolton, or, at least, the factory workers and the sound of their footsteps on the stone sidewalks was something one became accustomed to hearing. Clogs with their wooden soles and fitted with irons were considered to be very sensible footwear. Warm to the feet in the winter and delightfully cool to wear in the summer. They were also comparatively inexpensive.

The irons were malleable, 5/16" wide and 3/16" thick and were nailed around the edges of the soles and the heels, with small broad-headed nails counter sunk. The irons were in various sizes according to the sizes of the clogs, and being malleable, they were very easily hammered into shape.

These were what took the wear, but if replaced regularly, clogs had a long life of constant use.

The uppers were of good quality leather decorated with shiny, brass-headed tacks and toe-caps. They usually had clip fasteners to match, or they could be laced. Children wore them to school and were expected to keep them polished, with the aid of blacking. Often, when a girl or boy who normally had clogs, turned up at school wearing shoes, they were considered uppish and were often ridiculed.

So the Co-op cloggers' was a busy place in those days, especially at week-ends when there was some money flying about. If it was boots or shoes you wanted repairing, Mr Turner, the manager, would attend to you, give you a receipt and tell you when they would be ready. The same procedure if your clogs required re-clogging, you had to leave them.

But if it was only new irons you wanted, the manager would give you a small tin token on which a number was stamped, either, 1, 2, 3, or 4, according to how many irons you required, there being four irons to a set.

You paid the manager for the work to be done, then you went into the workshop to wait your turn. This is what took the time, your wait could be a short one, or a very long one, depending on how many people were waiting. It was usually a scene of great activity, three or four workmen sitting round the bench, all hammering away!

I remember being fascinated watching the man shaping the wood with the huge cutting tool. There were several of these tools hanging on the wall, they were about 4' 6" long. The man wore a heavy leather apron as protection. He very quickly shaped the block into a perfect clog sole.

There was a great deal of good-natured squabbling as to whose turn it was and if you could have listened you may have heard:-
"Neaw then," says a workman, "Stop that rackit, thet allus natterin'. Neaw, whose turn is it?"
"It's mine!" cries one lad.
"Me fust, a'wur 'ere afore thee!" protests another.
The clogger singles out one young boy who has been quiet. " 'Ere giv'us thi' tally.Wot dust waunt? wheer's thi' clugs? A'see, a set 'uv irons."
The boy hands over the two clogs and the clogger examines them closely. There is something about one of them that claims his attention.
At that moment, another older boy who is hugging a pair of clogs in one hand and eating a thick bread and jam butty with the other, exclaims:- "That mon's gone eaut 'uv 'is turn, a'wur in 'ere lung 'afore 'im, 'ees not bin in fahve minits."
The clogger looks up at him, "Sithee," says the workman, "thee let thi' meaut stop thi' gob, or else theau'll be in 'ere aw day."
The clogger holds clog he has been examining in his hand and turns to the young boy. "Sithee young fella', 'as thi' mother seen this crack?"
The boy hesitates a little before answering, "Aye, 'un oo'sed a'wur to tak' no 'eed ov it."
"Tak' no 'eed ov it? Tak' no 'eed ov it". he repeats. "What the 'eck is she talking abeaut? What's good o' purring' a new set ov irons on a clug that's beaunt faw i'to ony day?"
He hands the damaged clog back to the boy.
"'Al tell thi' wot,." says the clogger gently, "Thee tak' this clug back wum, and tell thi' mother warra' sed, 'al 'owd this other clug fer thi' til' theau comes back 'un tells mi' wot she sez."
The boy beats a hasty retreat taking the cracked clog with him.
"Neaw then, 'oos next?" says the clogger.
A young woman hands over a pair of large workman's clogs.
"Ah'd like a set ov irons, please." The clogger takes them from her and examines them.
"By gum, them's big 'uns. Ah've seen summat like thuse gliding deauwn t'canal loaded wi' coal. Ar'thi thi' faythur's?"
The young lady is not amused and does not reply.
"Nay durn't tak' offence, lass." "The clogger says smiling, "Ah wur' only kiddin' ".
The dialogue continues and so does the work of repairing.

Fred Hampson succeeded Mr Turner as manager. I well remember him being very stern and officious, in his dark suit and long, black apron reaching down to his toes. But, all in all, a visit to the cloggers was always enjoyable.

These happy hours have a sadness about them too, as William McDowell has found:-

WAITING FOR CLOG IRONS

Mrs. Brindle and her neighbours
In chapel-going Sunday black,
Were primly monumental.
But comelier far when,
Wearing a snowy brat with bib and tucker
Over a gay-striped factory skirt
And, easy in stocking feet,
They sat together on the clog-shop form.
Large blue and white checked cloths
That held fresh, crusty Co-op loaves
Lay on the floor beside them.
While, to the cobbler's rhythmic tap,
They held a willing-captive boy
With speech peppered with words
Our spinster teachers thought too coarse:
Wick, fettle, nesh, fawse, wichert and agate.
And phrases, too, that held a pithy charm—
Back-end, better than like, hoo'll clog agen.
"Yon little lad favvers yore Frank," one says,
and lays a rough, compassionate hand
On Mrs. Brindle's sturdy shoulder:
While tears well in each other's eyes
For the fair-quiffed lad who once sat here,
With shining, school-inspected clogs,
But died in heavy Army boots
Caked hard with bloodied Flanders mud.

I have been impressed that anyone whose father or grandad was a clogger is terribly proud of it. And rightly so. I'm fiercely proud of my grandad's bricklaying when I see the lovely wall around Rishton Cricket Club. He built it (single-handed I used to think) and it is simply a pride in the finished product of a real craftsman. The next few poems were written by people who share this pride.

T' LITTLE CLUGGERS SHOP (by Margaret Helliwell)

Below the house at number nine, ther wer a cluggers shop,
Weer aw went ter get mi irons on an aw allus ad ter stop.

An wait til thi wer finished, thi wor th' ony pair aw owned,
An awd goo wi foorpence i' mi hond, an goo an sit on't stooan.

Ther were aw meks o' stuff in theer, all ung i' links an rows,
An leather ung i' bundles, an fancy clugs on show
An't smell o't smook an leather, near knocked yer off yer feet
Th'owd chap werked in a kind o' haze, it wor a funny seet.

Ther'd bi two or three ats sat on't stooan, Wi hoiles in theels o't socks
An sum wiout any socks at all an sum i' cotton frocks.
An wid kick each others ankles, til 'e saidut we mun stop.
Or else e'd stop 'is warking, an chuck us owt ut shop.

Wi darnt goo whom wiout um dun so we ad tu settle dahn
An stare abart int shop instead or else wi gate a frown.
Awst tell thi muther ovver thee young Charlie he ud say
An friten livin daylights owt o' little Charlie Gray.

E'd bang an tap an chuckle an say just luke thi here
An ther wer a pair o' fancy clugs stood on a Windsor cheer.
Thi were small an thi wer pointed wi luvly ribbon lugs
Pale blue wi real brass studs in real fancy dancin clugs.

E' med um fer Dan Leno i med fower pair a year
An e'd deed afore e'd bowt um, so e'd kept um safly theer
Then e'd say now weer's thi fowerpence clugs is dun naw get thi whom
An away we'd all goo strickin sparks on't cobbles as we run.

MI GRANDFEYTHER WERE A COBBLER (by Marian Turner)

Mi grandfeyther were a cobbler
Aye, un mi feyther too
Monny a time awve gone in shop
Tu wattch him mend a shoe.

There were no sewin machines
He stitched wi awl un thread
He wore a barm skin pinny
Wi his glasses perched ut top of his yed.

His bench were cluttered wi awe so'urts o things
Hommers, pinchers un nails in tins
Uppers un iorns awe shapes un sizes
Fastened on tu bench were a coupl o' vices.

Ut one end ut shop were blades in a stock
Fro a lump o wood a sole he would shape
Thick uns, thin uns, hollow or flat,
What soart he wanted, he'd make.

While he were cutting, shavins would drop
Pilin up into a heap,
Curly and white, smellin sweet
Fawin awe areawnd his feet.

He made his own tachin end
By gum it were strung
Un laces for tall up shoon
He caw'd um leather thung.

Wi th'iron foot between his legs
He'd nail uppers tu tops,
Tekin nails fro his mouth
Yu'd uf thowt he'd swallow'd lot.

Foak would cum fri miles areaend
Tu buy his clogs fur dancing
Others would weer um on Sunday
Just to go'a swankin.

When awe wattched him mak um
Mi heart would fill wi pride
Fancy patterns un tu uppers
Brass studs awe reawnd side.

But neaw they're bo'eth de'ad un gone,
Un wi um de'ed their trade
Fur what few clogs are made neaw
Are only machine made.

Aye times hev awthered
Foaks hev changed their ways,
But clog makin were a werk of art
In my grandfeyther's day.

MI DAD'S SHOP (by Peter Thornley)

Mi dad wur t'local clogger wi' a shop at th' end o' t' street,
An' ayf o't'tahwn relied on 'im fur summat o' thur feet.
Th'd bring thur clogs an' boots an' shoon, thur case-baws in fro' t' schoo'
An' aw agreed thur wurn't a thing mi faythur couldn't do.

Dad's tools wur 'ommers, rasps an' knives an' awls t'poo an' thrust,
'e'd rows o' tins wi' lables on tha couldn't si fur dust,
An' boxes full o' laces, coulert eyelets clasps an' tongues,
An' bends o' leather aw tied up wi' proper leather thongs.

Yon cahwnter bulged wi' boots an' shoon, tha'd scarce believe thi e'en,
Fro' babby boot t'tharteen fuut an' ev'ry size between.
'e'd paint an' polish ev'ry sole an' trim aw th' edges neat,
Thi luuked that weeal id wur a shame t' weear 'em o' thi feet.

Dad geet aw sooarts o' customers, some good'n's an' some bad,
An' thur wur allus tuthri folk med faythur raythur mad.
Bad payers, penny pinchers too an' them wi' sweaty feet,
An' some 'at theawt dad ought t' wark aw day an' ayf o' t' neet.

One mon wur reg'lur to eawr shop, weeal reg'lar once a year,
An' t' state 'at yon mon's clogs wur in med faythur cuss an' swear.
'is cokers 'ad geet dahwn t' t' grahwnd an' t' wood wur wurrin' thin,
W'en axt if 'e could save 'em dad said "Aye ah con, fur t' bin."

Wi geet a fella in fro' t' mill cawd 'erbe't, 'oo wur lame,
'r theawt 'e wur, till fayther said "Tha foo', id's yon t' blame,
Tha's double cokers o' one clog, on t'other tha's geet none,
Tha'll 'av' t' walk wi' one leg stuck in t' gutter if tha con".

Dad allus liked t' gi' folk 'ond if 'e could see 'is way,
An of'en leet 'em off wi' t' bill if prawce thi couldn't pay,
Ad least that's wad Ah theawt 'e did but then Ah'm raythur thick,
Ah should 'a known 'e'd get 'is brass plus ten per cent fur tick.

Ah'v geet fond mem'ries o' yon shop 'fooar t' business getten slack,
Bud t' mills closed dahwn an' folk left tahwn, wi never geet 'em back,
Id's years nah sin' thi poo'd t'place dahwn bud sometimes late at neet,
Ah'll sweear Ah con 'ear t' sahwnd o' 'ammerin' in t' street.

I like to think that Edwin Waugh, that prince—neah, king,—of Lancashire writers, had a clogger in mind when he wrote this next poem. How I'd love to see one of our Lancashire folk-song groups putting this to music:

HEIGHO FOR COBBLERS

Of all the craftsmen in this world,
The cobbler lad for me,
With his pegs an' tacks, an' his hemp an' wax,
An' his lapstone on his knee.
Welt it, an' pelt it;
Pelt it, an' welt it:
Sing, heigho for cobblers!

The lads that patch these poor men's shoon,
I fain would have you know,
They are the friends on whom depends
What footing you must go.
Twitch it, an' stitch it;
Stitch it, an' twitch it;
Sing, heigho for cobblers!

Saint Crispin was a lad of wax,
And he tugged the 'tachin-end;
And he plied his awl in his good old stall,
The soles of men to mend:
Stump it, an' clink it;
Clink it, an' stump it;
Sing, heigho for cobblers!

Then, here's good luck to the old cow's hide,
Likewise the good lapstone;
The man whose footsteps never slide,
Shall seldom need to moan:
Ring it, an' ding it;
Ding it, an' ring it;
And, heigho for cobblers!

The man that keeps his top-knot cool
Will never come to harm,
If he gets a lad with a leather-brat
To keep his poor feet warm:
Thump it, an' stump it;
Stump it, an' thump it;
Sing, heigho for cobblers!

Good luck attend the cobbler's awl,
His hemp, an' nails, an' tacks,—
His knife, an' last , an' blackin'-ball,
His bristles, an' his wax!
'Tach it, an' catch it;
Catch it, an 'tach it;
Sing, heigho for cobblers!

And when, at last, he quits his awl,
And lays him down to rest,
He shall sleep sound 'neath a grassy mound
With a lapstone on his breast:
End it, an' mend it;
Mend it, an' end it;
Sing, heigho for cobblers!

The early Lancashire poets must have seen cobblers as patient old men. Perhaps they too were looking through the eyes of a child. Remember that Sam Laycock, telling us about his neighbours in Bowton's Yard, says:-

At number nine th' owd cobbler lives - th' owd chap at mends mi shoon
He's getting very weak an' done, he'll ha' to leov us soon;
He reads his Bible every day, an' sings just like a lark,
He says he's practisin' for heaven - he's welly done his wark.

Local historian John Cassidy observed the demolition of Bowton's Yard in Stalybridge and it seemed only right that No 9 was the last to go. The Lord must have remembered him.

William Baron (Bill o' Jacks, 1865-1927), a Rochdale poet shared the same view of the cobbler:-

TH' OWD COBBLER

Th' owd cobbler's well liked bi his nayburs, -
He patches an' mends o ther shoon;
He sings th' long day throo o'er his labours,
An' allus to some merry tune.
No matter whenever yo' see him,
He's at it fro' mornin' to neet;
It fair does one good to be wi' him,
For his nature's so sunny an' breet.

He luvs to "rive eawt", as he co's it,
For melody flows in his veins;
Content fills his heart, an' he shows it
Bit th' gladness 'at rings throo his strains.
"This world's nooan so bad as folks reckon",
Aw've mony a time yerd him say;
"An' yo know not when Deeath's hond may beckon,
Sooa try to mek th' best o' yor stay".

He ne'er looks ahead to seech sorrow,
For he larnt, long ere reychin' his prime,
'At most joy fro' life we con borrow
Bi livin' one day at a time.
Wi' him, as wi' th' rest o' poor mortals,
Things neaw an' then gooa a bit wrong;
But when trubble enters his portals
He chases it eawt wi' a song.

Th' owd cobbler's as blithe as a cricket -
No minit i' th' day he finds dull,
An' till th' scythe-bearer bowls deawn his wicket,
He'll enjoy life's innings to th' full.
He cares nowt for fame's empty bubble,
No riches hes he to tek wings;
But a mon 'at con sing away trubble
Is one to be envied bi kings.

Stalybridge poet Reg Palmer, whose pen-name is Lan Castria, writes short verses to act as an introduction to his work and has published them to good effect:

THE CLOGMAKER

When Lancashire meant cotton mills,
And chimney smoke meant fogs,
And decayed teeth meant toothache,
Snow and slush meant clogs.

THE CLOGMAKER

Owed Jim, 'e was a clogger
Wi a workshop, up some steps,
Ther'l be lots o' folk a warin,
Those fancy clogs 'e meks.

'e cuts the soles from wooden blocks,
Wi a fancy shaped machine,
An clever folk 'ave coed it,
A clogger's guillotine.

An wen 'es finished shapin' soles,
An tacked 'is leather round,
'e's ready then fer buckle in,
An' pattin' toe-caps down.

A can see 'im now a shapin'
Some very pointed soles,
'e ses ther for a clog-dancer,
'o puts on special shows.

An' then thers bread and butter clogs,
Which Jim meks by the score,
An' when ther blacked and polished up,
Ther ready for the store.

But one thing's sure, ther is no doubt,
For warin on yer feet,
Yo canna beat Jim's wooden clogs
Becos ther made just reet.

Brian Clare finds joy, sadness and pride in his poem:-

MI TRADE

He sat in't shed ut bottum ut yard
Us dayleet slowly faded.
Uh little tyert, owdish mon,
He favert proper jaded.

His calloused hond't lied on his knee,
It twitch't frum time tu time,
Us if it wantit wark ugen, but cudn't,
Wi its mesther past his prime.

He slowly raise't his snow white yed
He rubbed his waytherin een,
Un us he gazet tut gatherin gloom
He thowt uh what heed been.

A likely lad when in his teens,
In't war he answert caw,
Un waatch't his mates dee raewnd him,
It wer freetnin tu recaw.

When it were oer he coom back wom,
Un settle't daewn tu wark,
He knew he had some graftin't do
If he had fert make his mark.

Uh clugger bi trade, he wer busy then
As he made un sowd his wares
Clugs fert pit un clugs fert mill
He made mony uh hundhert pairs.

A lass cawd Mary coom on't scene
It seeum't us it wer fate,
Inside three months ut mooest
He'ed took her fer his mate.

Two bonny childer blest ther wom
Uh sturdy lad, uh pratty lass,
Th' happiness he had just then
He never thowt wud fade un pass.

But pass it did un't childer went
One wed un one in't graewnd,
His missus to, her wer tan
Un lonelyness he faewnd.

Ney ut nigh on eighty six,
His life were empty sad un done,
He'ed had enoof uh livin,
He wer ready fert gu wum.

Un us he look't raewnd t' darknin shed,
His dusty tools he spied.
On 't flooer ugen his feet,
Uh clug lay on its side.

Slowly then he raiset his yed,
His face creaset in uh smile,
Fear uh deein left his heart
He thowt uh little while.

When he geet tut Gowd'n Gate,
Un God he had fert see,
He'ed ask, polite but humble like,
Is ther uh place fer me?

Yo help't yer Dad ut carpentin
Us he his livin made
So yu'll understond ma soart uh mon,
Am fro Lancashire, un cluggin wer mi trade.

Josephine Iddon's memories are only fond ones of:-

TH' OWD CLOGGER

Mi Mams been a' bowt me some new clogs today,
Cos t' others were 'urting mi toes,
Oo geet 'em at Ashtons i' Leyland Looan,
He's a gradely good clogger tha knows,
He's o sooarts o clogs, he does piles o repairs,
Mam says he makes monny a pound,
Ah like callin' theer on mi way hooam fro' t' schoo',
Ah've to wait while he irons me o round.

As Ah sit theer on t' stoo' in his little shop,
If Ah ax 'How long will you be'?,
He says 'Ah'm five feet four in mi stockin' feet,
An' Ah knows he's teasin' me.

He's allus some chocolate an' tuffee to eat,
An' t' tales as he tells make me smile,
Ah'm missin' o this now Ah've gettan new clogs,
Ah've no need to call for a while.

Fond too are the memories of Louisa Bearman. You can hear her recite her "Clogger's shop" poem on Big Ben Records BB.00.06 and read it in her book "Poems in the Lancashire Dialect" (Dalesman 1977).

CLUGGER'S SHOP

Aaw youst goo every Sat'day morn
When mi Muther geet Dad's pay:
Her'd say, "Gerr off to clugger's-
And durn't sit theere aaw day."

Her'd tek her clugs fro' off her feet
Un' Aaw'd put one on each hand,
Un' clap um gether aaw deawn t'street
Like a drummer in a band.

Aaw loved gooing up ta clugger's,
Mi mates ud all bi theere
Sittin' on an owd woodbench
Un' clugger in his chee-er.

Shop had a smell aw of its own
O' wood, un 'ile, un' leather,
Un' smook uz blew deawn chimbney oile,
Especially in rough weather.

We'd sit theere in eawr stockin' feet
Wi' big toes peepin' through,
Un' then we'd kick each others' legs
Fer want o' summat do.

Clug irons hung fro' ceiling hook
Tied wi' a piece of string,
Un' wi'd rattle um un' shek um
Till it made thi yerholes ring.

Eh, clugger we a patient mon
E're awmost deef un' dumb,
Fer th' only words I yerd him say
Wer, "Wheere's brass, clugs are done."

Most cloggers were known simply as " t' clogger", but Elizabeth Morris remembers the name of her's:

WHERE ARE YOU NOW, EDDIE BROWN?

When the clog-irons were worn down, they could be replaced either by nailing on new ones at home, or by taking them to be 'clogged' at the clogger's. The clogger's shop was at the street corner. It smelt of leather and iron filings. The door was propped open, appropriately enough, with a last. You could sit, clogless, on a bench seat running the length of one wall, while the operation was performed. A pile of well worn comics was provided for you to while away the time. Sometimes by good fortune you could turn up a Skipper or a Wizard among the comics. Grown men would sit reading the comics as well as children.

Behind the counter sat Eddie Brown, his workshop bounded by the counter, the dusty shop window, the rear wall shelved and hooked and laden, and a door to the mysterious private living room behind. From time to time this door opened, admitting Eddie's mysterious quiet wife, wearing a crossover floral pinafore and carrying a pint pot of tea, which she set on a ledge behind the counter and as mysteriously vanished through the door. On the shelves were boxes of tacks and brassheaded nails, tins of blacking, tins of dubbin and dark brown cakes of cobblers' wax. Piles of leather clog uppers and wooden soles waited to be made up. Cards offered for sale packets of nails, and twists of oiled thread, and tubes of Stick-it-fast, and other cards advertised brands of polish. Two lines stretching the length of the shop held the irons, one the heel irons like miniature horseshoes, the other the sole irons, elongated and curved. They ranged in size from the small children's at one end to the great men's at the other.

Eddie Brown sat in his little shop window, tap-tap-tapping the nails and forming the irons to the curve of the soles of the clogs, or stitching away at his sewing machine with its clattering treadle. He wore a leather apron, and a waistcoat over his union flannel shirt, and nails in his mouth. His shirt was collarless, open at the neck, sleeves rolled up to the elbows. He was deep-chested, broad-shouldered, and laconic, perhaps by reason of the nails in his mouth.

Conversations here were conducted in staccato phrases by adults, male and serious, on subjects such as cricket and distant wars. Under Eddie's heavy-browed gaze, children's chatter was suppressed and low-toned. It was there I learned of Leary Constantine and

Eddie Paynter, as well as of lesser local heroic figures, and of things happening in Germany and Russia, and India which consisted of dark-skinned men wearing clothing of white cotton cloth woven at the bottom of our street but wanting to weave their own.

In pride of place in Eddie's shop were two pairs of miniature clogs, each about three inches from heel to toe. One was red, with bright brassheaded nails, the other royal blue and decorated with a filigree pattern of punched holes, models of clogs for dancing. It must have been some perverse kind of determination that made people think of dancing in such heavy and clumsy wear as clogs. However a champion clog-dancer was far from clumsy, and tapped out a lively rhythm on cobbles or flags outdoors or on a slatted wooden mat indoors.

Clogs were highly prized possessions, and to keep them bright and shining a point of honour. Women's and children's were fastened with a strap and stud, men's and boys' with a massive buckle. A boy's first pair of buckled clogs was as significant as, and earlier than, long trousers, at the age of about nine I think but may be wrong. At eleven I put away childish things and went to the big school.My clogs were replaced with shoes. Long black stockings—and an awareness of my dignity as a young lady—insulated my legs from the flagstones and my thoughts from the street.

* * * *

There was one aspect of the clogger's work that I didn't touch upon in "Concerning Clogs", and that was the sizes of clogs and the fact that they don't co-incide with shoe sizes, or rather they didn't use to do, because now it is common to use only one measurement. Why it was so, I don't truly know, but in years past—certainly up to the 1950's in my own experience—shoe sizes from "Child's Clog" to "Child's 10", were increased by two when converted to "Child's Clog" sizes, then the 11 converted to size 1, 12 to size 2, 13 to size 3. After that came "Adult 1 (shoe) which converted to (clog size) 4 and from there onwards, shoe sizes were converted to clog sizes by adding a figure 3. A little confusing perhaps, but generations of cloggers managed nicely with the system. For information on this I am indebted to Walter Hirst, still clogging in Hindley.

Doris Lord recalls her mother sending her to the cloggers and how she wore out her new irons. Although re-ironing was not expensive (due to competition keeping prices down), it was an expense that parents considered unnecessarily incurred:

THI' CLOGS NEED ARNIN'

"Thi clogs need arnin' an' ther's meyt to fotch,—Lady!"
Mi mam allus calls me "Lady" when hoo's vexed.
Wi' a luk at't clock Ah thowt "Lat fer't schoo' agen!"
Sooer fingers agen 'cos o't meyt an't clogarns.

Bai lad, yon teycher cud lay on wi' yon ruler, wen hoo wanted!! Onyway, id wer't big bakin' day - Thursday - an' wen Ah coom wom ther'd be't breyd an't mowfins, an't tato pie, mi mam wer so gud at, an't kitchen 'ud be so hot, laik Owd Nick's cellar.
David the clogger, meuth foo o' nayls, tap, tap, bangin' arns to shape on his last, an' suppin' tay eaut o' a big mug every neau an' then. How slow he seems - - - tap, tap, - - - seven nayls to a front arn, an' fower to a heel - - - tap, tap, - - -.
"Wod taym is't David? - - Ah've to get this yer meyt wom, an' ged to't schoo!!"
"Calm thisel' deaun, Ah corn'd do 'em ony faster!"
- - - Soon - - -
"Theer tha'art, neauw, that's sevenpence ho'p'ny."
Clatter, clatter eaut o't shop.
"Must kick a few sparks wi' mi neauw arns, on't flags, but Ah'd better nod ged copped or Ah'll ged belted! Speshully wi' mi neauw un's - - Ah ged better sparks wen Ah'm runnin'."
Soon as Ah'm wom Ah dump t'meyt on't table, an' fly to't schoo', bud Ah corn'd escape thad ruler, Onyway, Ah'll a' to led thad tato pie an' rice puddin' mek up fer id, at dinnertime!
- - - Ah wunder, - - - 'ow wer id thad mi clogs wanted arnin' on't same mornin' Ah'd't meyt to fotch??

Similarly, Mary Jane Findon has fond memories of her visits to the clog-shop:

OWD JOHN, THE CLOGGER MON

Mi flippin' clog ud worn its iron.
"Oh, No. Oh God", Ah groaned.
"Ah 'ope mi Dad dunt spil mi sport
Wi' t' leather strips." Ah moaned.

Ah 'ated leather strips on t' clogs.
Thi spoilt mi fun an' games.
Not only that, thi stopped mi gooin'
To t' cloggers just down t' lane.

Ah loved gooin' t' clogger's
To 'ave new irons on t' clogs.
We'd sit on t' counter, un mess about,
In t' stockin' feet un t' socks.

"Next" John ud shout, an' in we'd march,
Wi' t' clogs in eawr 'ond,
An' sit an' feast eawr beady eyes
On John, eawr clogger mon.

Wooden roller from th' owd mangle
Served John's purpose right.
It stood upright between 'is legs,
Wi' t' last jammed well in tight.

An' t' nails 'e stuffed well in his mouth
Saved time, 'e allus 'arped.
Fost time Ah watched Ah froze on t' spot,
In case 'e swallowed 'ard.

On mi clogs, when done, Ah'd gaze in awe,
An' 'ug 'em to mi breast.
The stand-up blue-grey irons
Ah knoo 'ud serve me best.

Them soundless, soggy leather strips
Ah 'ated wi mi 'eart.
"So please, God, please, don't let me Dad
Tek away mi larks."

The economics of the clog-trade and the household are brought out in Evelyn Swarbrick's poem:

ERE'S THI CLOGS

Am back fray cloggers, an dust no,
Av geet em dun but thow'd so an so
Wanted brass an wouldna wait
A toothri days for Arry's mate
To gi us wot he owes i rent.
I sed I corn't get clog irons lent.
He sed "bod foos'll work for nowt"
I mun av to pay an nod just nowt.
If I hadn't gin im o' is pay
Tha wouldnta getten thi clogs today.

Nora Hodgkinson's father was a clogger (her pen-name is "Clogger's Dowter") and this has made her think deeply on clogs:

CLOGS

Babby's clogs, i' black 'n' red,
Lickle feet were dancin' led,
Ta mek a noiz, soa mam cud 'eer
Babby's wandrins' fer 'n' neer.

Childer's clogs, wi strap 'n' clasp,
Punch'd-eaut toaz, an' cawkers rasp

'long t' flag-stoans, mekkin' sparks.
Lads 'n' lasses, eaut fer larks.

Grown-up clogs, fer t' fooak a t' mill,
Standin' weyvin' aw eaurs, til,
Geddin' ooam, afoor ther tay,
Thid polish t' clogs fer wark nex day.

Owd fooaks clogs, thi av ta last
Mony a winter, safe fra t' blast
Wi gud clog-soyls an' uppers ruff,
S'no wonder northern fooaks wer tuff.

Clogs, clogs, fermilyer seaunds
O t' knocker-ups clogs, wen, on is reaunds
Rat-tattin' ut winders in t' cowd 'n' dark,
Powl under th' arm, eed bin up wi t' lark.

Th'ooters piercin' scream fra t' mill,
Summons t' warkers 'genst ther will,
Noizy, chattrin' craads, bedogg'd
Bi noizier, clattrin', seaund o' clogs.

Ah've sin clogs 'angin' deawn fra th'ooks,
Th'all nod si thad i' th'istry books,
'cos t' clogger - wer a gradely lad,
Ah'll sweer ta thad - id wer mi dad.

Ah've sin 'im wi'is back bent double,
Sweatin', thrutchin', face wi stubble,
Muscles writhin', cuttin', purrin',
Shapin' t' wud fer t' soyls ta wurrin'.

Knives ud flash, afoor thi een
Lumps o' wud fly in-between
T' benches, spred wi nails o' brass,
Tools o' trade fer t' warkin' class.

'ommers, pinchers, bits o' leather,
Match-stems, chalk, aw mix'd tagether,
'tachin-end, ta cover-up th'oyl,
'is eyd bent deawn, i' 'onnist toyl.

Snotty-noas'd kids, in t'stockin' feet,
Moar feet than stockin', ev'ry neet
Thid sit on t'bench, an' feight an' sheaut
Fer t' comics thad mi dad dish'd eaut.

T'days wark dun, e'ed reych fer t'briar
An' throw "Wud-chips" on top o' t'fire,
Jus' fer a minit t' flames ud leap
Like orange tongs, then sink ta t' deep.

Days lon' gon', th'yll ne'er cum back,
Fer cloggin' is a deein' 'nack,
Mi dad med one mistake - it's done,
'e 'ed a dowter - sted ov a son.

Ta-day, strange fooak fra fer-off lands,
Wark in t'mill as extra 'ands,
Thiv neether sin nor 'eerd o' clogs,
Alas, King Cotton's gon ta t' dogs.

A man engaged in the clogging trade yet about whom little is known so far as his working conditions are concerned is the clog-block maker, often called the itinerant bodger (though bodger/badger is a word that seems to have been applied to any sort of person who travelled the countryside plying a trade. A lady has told me of a "hen badger", who came round the farmsteads buying and selling hens). I mentioned these chaps in "Concerning Clogs", and suggest for further reading an excellent article by Reg Barlow in "*Lancashire Life*" October 1978. "Straight from the wood" tells of Reg's father's working conditions amongst the alder trees, preparing blocks of wood from the cut trees so that some clog-shop clogger could create from them the sole to fit the leather upper.

Another excellent article which appeared in "*Lancashire Life*" (March 1978) was simply called "*The Clogger*" by Matt Glenn, recalling his days on the tools. His use of one word started a discussion amongst other cloggers. The world was "*laths*", which were the razor-sharp tools used to slice through wooden blocks when sole-cutting. This seems to have been a localised (in Ashton-u-Lyne) word, as most cloggers called them "*stock-knives*" or "*cloggers' knives*". There were three types, each having a different-shaped cutting head for a specific job. They were "*the stock-knife*", "*the hollower*" and "*the gripper*".

3. Clog Dancing

It annoys me when people describe the Morris-type of troupe dancers as clog-dancers because they happen to wear clogs. Let's get it right—clog-dancers are individuals dancing intricate steps in clogs. Tap-dancing evolved from clog-dancing. Some of the best-known tap-dancers and artistes started as clog-dancers, Charlie Chaplin, Ernie Wise, Stan Laurel, Little Tich and Hylda Baker. The king of them all was Dan Leno, who proudly could call himself The World Champion Clog Dancer. It is a hundred years since he won that title, but his memory lives on. There has been some disbelief of the story that the judges in the dancing contests of that period actually sat *under* the stage to listen to the dancers' feet rather than watching them dance, but Dan Leno's son, Herbert Dan has verified that this was so. In a letter to the Daily Telegraph (8.1.1978), young Dan sets a couple of other matters right:

I am very amazed at the letters that have been coming in about my father, Dan Leno. The letter from M.L. Minty (Dec. 18th) has now prompted me to write the true facts about my father. He could not be classed in any way with Albert Chevalier, Whimsical Walker or Little Tich as he was a character comedian and dressed accordingly for every character with patter to match. He never included his championship clog dance in his routines but at the end of his act he would change his clothes and put on his clogs (at the side of the stage while the band played) and would then do his championship dance by request of the audience. He never worked his act from a script, but extemporised, which L.M. Minty probably thought was confusion. He never wore his clogs in his championship acts.

He did not die in a lunatic asylum, but at his home "Springfield", Atkins Road, Clapham Park. He was working at the Pavilion Music Hall, London on October 21st, 1904 where he was taken ill and was driven home in his own carriage with his son John to "Springfield" where he died of heart failure on October 31st, 1904.

I am 85 years old and remember from 1901-4 every detail of my father's life as though it was yesterday.

Herbert Dan Leno
Ewell, Surrey

As I said, Dan Leno lives on. There is now a great movement in the country towards learning clog-dancing. And not just in the Northern counties. If there is one man who has brought this about his name is Sam Sherry, a diminutive dancer with feathers for feet. Sam's father, James Bernard Sherry, ('Dan Conroy'), was a contemporary of Leno, self-taught in step dancing. He told Sam about the famous Leeds and Oldham championships, and there was a signed Dan Leno photo in their home. Sam and his brothers were taught clog dancing in a traditional style, - Lancashire clog steps. As times had changed when Sam started on the halls, he danced tap rather than clog, and recalls that only one man, a Yorkshire comedian called Walter Nibbler, used clog dancing in his act. Times changed further, music hall declined and Sam came out of the business in 1955. Four years later he joined a Lancaster folk club. Within a short time he had bought a pair of clogs and volunteered to dance at the club. Within a short time he was dancing for the English Folk Dance & Song Society in London, and soon afterwards teaching his craft at Folk Festivals. At this time, a clog-dancing revival had occurred in the North East under the legendary Johnson Elwood. (There are technical differences between Lancashire steps and Durham/Northumberland steps). Sam started teaching classes of eager pupils at Lancaster in the early 70's, and later started a Preston class too. There are now thousands of Sherry-trained lads and lasses throughout the country, all of whom have been told, "Practice is vitally important". He has run workshops at Folk Festivals at Taunton, Southampton, Reading, Bournemouth, Chelmsford as well as Durham and Fleetwood. A 16mm film on Sam's dancing can be hired from E.F.D.S.S., Cecil Sharp House, London NW1 (Tel. 01 485 2206).

After 2 years of holding "The Lancashire and Cheshire Clog Dancing Championship" (both of which were won by Alan Fletcher, one of Sam's pupils from Lancaster) at Fleetwood, Sam initiated a "clog waltz competition", after some debate over the strictness of the "off-the-toe" style of the traditional Lancashire style. This will allow competitors to express themselves freely and allow their originality to come out. At the 1980 Fylde Folk Festival most of the competitors danced to the old tune "Daisy". It is expected that more people will enter this particular competition, thus helping to keep folk a-clogging. Long may Sam Sherry delight us.

A poem that I'm particularly fond of, as it has built-in clog-dancing rhythm as well as delightful words and sentiment is this one by Eric Holt. It has been set to music and performed by a Chorley-based folk group, *The Blue Water Folk:*

JUMPIN' JACK

Watch 'im goo, yon gradely prancer,
Tappin' toes, an' clackin' 'eels,
Jumpin' Jack, 'ee's best clug dancer,
E'er stepped eawt wi' jigs an' reels.

Twistin', turnin', peawndin', prancin',
Wile th' owd fiddle sings away,
Leeter than a fither dancin'
On a breeze i' t' month o' May.

Watch yon childer clap together,
Keepin' time to t' click an' clack,
Summer, Winther, onny weather,
Eawt thi coom to Jumpin' Jack.

Carnivals corn't do wi' eawt 'im,
Churches want 'im for t' bazaars,
O'er Sixties weren't bi beawt 'im,
Sooner 'im ner t' telly stars.

Pair on pair o' clugs 'ee's batthered,
Still 'is pins er sthraight an' thrue,
As on t' day when 'ee fust clatthered,
I' new clugs when 'ee were two.

Jack lad, keep thi toes i' fettle,
Mak' eawr spirits gay an' leet,
Though thi clugs be shod wi' metal,
Wi find gowd i' them two feet.

Clog-dancing cannot be separated from the music hall, though apart from the Dan Leno period, the subject is not greatly recorded. What is apparent is that Lancashire plays a big part in the clog-dancing that there was in music halls. It was a Manchester lad, Charles Corlette, who wrested the championship from Dan Leno, and he was to star at the Queen's Theatre, Manchester. People wanted to see clog-dancers in the halls. Besides this, Corlette proudly stated "*...winner of the Championship of the World, 1901, 1902, 1903,....holder of the world's record of 211 steps (16 bars to a step) in 50 minutes ....Trick, Step, Sand, Coon, Top-boot, Clogs, Flap and all fancy dances taught....*" He also published "*The Universal Theatrical Stage Tutor and Guide*" from his Northern Theatrical Academy, Manchester. The Manchester Guardian, telling of his winning one of the World Championships recorded...

"The smart wooden soles gave out a pleasingly musical accompaniment to the agile manoeuvering of his twinkling feet. Just before the end the cinematograph machine buzzed softly as it recorded for future ages the finish of the contest." If only that film could be found. When he won the 50 minutes world record, he collected the largest stake ever danced for - £200. Therein may lie the reason why clog-dancers appeared in music halls - the public wanted to see them, were willing to pay to see them and so entrepreneurs would put money up knowing that they would recoup it.

I think you will enjoy reading *"The funniest man on earth - the story of Dan Leno"* by Gyles Brandreth (pub. 1977 by Hamish Hamilton).

The annual Durham Folk Festival has strong connections with clog-dancing. The judges for the competitions include Mary Jameson, daughter of Johnson Elwood, who carries on her father's craft by teaching. Another, Don Watson acts as collator for information on clogs and clog-dancing for all the country and edits the Durham Festival's "Clog News Sheet". Those lads and lasses dancing in heaven must be looking down and smiling that their beloved craft is being carried on.

At Durham and at Fleetwood, where Pat Stacey is the leading authority on the traditional Lancashire style (and hopes soon to publish a book on the old steps), the judges look and listen and mark for carriage/deportment, timing consistency, beat regularity and general execution. I listened in at the 1980 clog workshops at Fleetwood, hearing a valuable discussion between Sam Sherry, Pat Tracey, Don Watson, Mary Jameson and relative newcomers Sue Bousefield and Madeline Hollis (those last two had won competitions earlier that day) I asked "Why have these championships?" It was explained, *"They help set standards which will eventually be raised, and avoid simple showmanship."* Sam interjected *"Learners have to have something to aim for. Also, to do it just for one's own enjoyment is not enough, you need an audience or you will end up not enjoying it"*. Winding up the discussion, Sam, who takes pride in being called "Mr Clever Clogs", came out with - *"Dancing is a joyous thing"*. How right he was.

Whilst I have explained that clog-dancing has little or nowt to do with the Morris groups we see now, I hasten to add that these groups do a great job in preserving our English traditions and in awakening people to an awareness of clogs. Such a lad wrote this poem:

A' CLOGGING ALL THE DAY

On market days, when I was young,
Me dancin' gear came out,
Then me an't lads would stand in line
An' gather folks about.

We'd dance until our feet did ache,
Our clogs on't cobbles rang,
An' people stood t' watch us dance
An' 'ear t' songs we sang.
An' if t' weather turned to rain
An' folks all went away,
We'd only smile as we went on
A'cloggin' all the day.

Cloggin in the market square,
Thats the way we'd stay,
A singin' songs, a drinkin' ale
An' cloggin' all the day.

When Christmas time 'uld come around
A Wassailin' we'd go,
Trampin' round from 'ouse to 'ouse,
An' cloggin' through t' snow.
A party may be ruined when
Its raining cats an' dogs,
Then we cum round and dry the ground
By friction of t' clogs.
Many's the time we'd stay all neet
With good ale as our pay,
Suppin' 'til the early leet,
Then cloggin' all the day.

When Christmas time would come around,
That's the way we'd stay,
A singin' songs, a drinkin' ale,
An' cloggin' all the day.

An' when July Wakes arrived,
Those on decent pay,
'Uld pack their bags an' leave the town
For their weeks holiday.
But for those of us not so well off
Our week off for the year
Was spent in singin' in the square,
An' dancin' for us beer.
An' for a week we all would be
Happy, content and gay,
Lettin' neets just pass us by,
An' cloggin' all the day.

Aye, when July Wakes arrived,
That's the way we'd stay,
A singin' songs, a drinkin' ale,
An' cloggin' all the day.

But all these things were in me youth,
Now old age 'as me beat,
Its been ten year since I even 'ad
Me clogs upon me feet.
I sometimes sit and watch a group
Clog dancin' on the green,
It brings back memories fond and clear
Of things I've done and seen.
But now me limbs are stiff an' old,
An. now me hairs turned grey,
An't lads and me no longer go
A' cloggin' all the day.

But in deepest dreams at neet,
I know I'll always stay,
A singin' songs, a drinkin' ale,
An' cloggin' all the day.

A country dance band formed a few years ago wanted a name for themselves. They thought of "*Clogs*" but learned that there already was such a band, so they hit upon the idea of calling themselves after the clogshop where they bought their own dancing clogs. You can contact "*Clarkson's Clogs*" through George Downham, 12 Hillside Road, Lower Bentham, Lancaster. (Tel. Bentham 61860). Another group of folksong enthusiasts in Atherton also decided to incorporate clogs into their group name. One of the group, Dave Dutton, is a writer of comedy material and his influence is detected in their name - "*Inclognito*". Contact them through Bram Taylor, 64 Arlington Drive, Leigh (Tel. 602864). Their material has a very definite Lancashire bias.

4. Teachers of Clog Dancing

I have compiled this list of people who teach clog dancing. It is as accurate and as complete as I can make it, but not in any particular order.

Sam Sherry, 53 Meadow Park, Glagate, Lancaster (Tel 751785)
Sue Bousefield, 9, Thirlmere Avenue, Fleetwood (Tel 5127)
Vera Aspey, 29 Beech Walk, Leigh (Tel 671995)
Mary Jamieson, 13 Northlands, Chester-le-Street, Co. Durham
Rita Hewitt, 4, Barrow Lane, Hessle, Humberside.
Peter Brown, 6, Somerton Court, Kenton, Newcastle on Tyne (Tel 868265)

There are others, but I can't give full details as I don't have them. I suggest that anyone wanting to learn to clog-dance might get in touch with the organisers of the various Folk Festivals and ask who runs the clog-dancing workshops at the Festival. I'd be pleased to hear of any other teachers.

Above and opposite: Two attractive scraperfoil studies by Peter Wilkinson, Blackpool.

5. Odd Sizes

In this part of the book I am including poems and stories which don't fit into the other sections.

A PAIR O' DACENT CLOGS (by Harvey Kershaw)

There's nowt beats wearin' gradely clogs,
(Owd fashioned though they be)
Wear 'em when it's rainin' "Cats an' Dogs",
An' yo'll never witcherd be!

They're kind to t' feet; an' warm to t' toes,
Mich healthier nor shoon;
They'll noan cause corns, or bunion woes,
For warkers - they're a boon!

There's nowt to beat clogs on yo'r feet,
When thrang wi' gardenin' wark;
Comfort yo'll find, in cowd or heat,
Fro' morn, till th' edge o' dark!

Heawever rough yo'r wark mote be,
Heawever hard yo' plod,
What-e'er th' weather, yo' mun agree,
Wi' clogs, yo'r allus weel-shod.

Mill-warkers; Carters; Farmers too,
Prefer 'em to aught else;
Shoon for hard-wark, just winnot do!
So try clogs for yo'rsel's.

Then dunnot hobble i' tight shoon,
An' a tight-rope walk, like Blondin;
Good clogs yo'll find - o else aboon,
Provide gradely "under-stondin'.

MI CLOGS (by Joan Monaghan)

In a cupboard owd and ancient,
Rest two prized owd friends,
Black and shiny, friendly, patient,
Who'll stay wi me, until life ends.

You may say 'What's she on abeaut',
They're just a pair o' clogs.
That may be so but jus' fer me
They've bin as faithful as two dogs!

They've bin buffed an' scuffed, carved many
A scar. On legs boath live an' wooden
Fer puncin't polish off best cheer,
I've 'ad to goo beaut puddin!

Then later they took me to wark,
Clatterin' up yon hill.
Sometimes Ah still would mek 'um spark
An impulse to fulfil.

Then all the din went eaut o' them,
Like a roar takken eaut o' 't lions,
Co's mi Mam had 'ad um mended
Wi' new fangled rubber irons!

I wore 'um till Ah finished wark,
But they soon went eaut o' fashion
Wedge heels arrived an' caused a stir
When yer could get yer ration.

So in that cupboard weer they rest,
Sometimes I have a peep,
An' a'll swear they've grown an eye apiece,
That wink at me. Then close in sleep!

I mentioned earlier the pleasure that I had when in "Jacky Dummy's" shop in Manchester Road, Baxenden. Just up the road in a churchyard is something else which gives me pleasure. It reminds me of my grandma, who always wore clogs. It is a gravestone on which is shown an angel - in clogs. That was my grandma.

Mary Burge tells a nice tale about an owd chap and his clogs:-

OWD TOM'S CHOICE

'Wad ah remember moast abowt Tom wer his clogs. They

hed a shine on 'em as yo cud see yer face in, pointed toes they hed, they wer lace-ups and shod wi' irons. Thad wer in th' owd days afore they cum to be shod wi rubber.

Ah used to hear him go past mi dooar every neet on his way to wet his whistle and ah'd hear him cum back when t' pub wer shut. If mi dooar wer oppen he'd shout "good neet" as he went past. Id wer nice and friendly like.

Onny rooad, wun neet ah never eeard him nayther gooing nor cummin back.

"That's queer," ah thowt to missel, "it's not like Tom to miss his ale."

Ah listened, then ah peeked eawt o' t' dooar to see if his leet wer on but it weren't.

Ah wer curious and a bit bothered like in case he weren't so weel but onny rooad ah went to bed.

Next morning ah sees Tom tekkin his milk in.

"Mornin'" he ses.

"Mornin Tom, awreet are you?"

"Aye, nowt wrong wi' me lass."

That wer that but ah listened agen at neet and ah never heeard him go past, neyther that neet nor allweek. 'Appen he wer saving up.

Ah menshunned it to Ada at t' selling eawt shop when ah called theer afther tay.

"Owd Tom must be stopping in at neet," ah ses.

"Wad meks thi say that?" ses Ada half smiling.

"Well," ah ses, "ah allus hear him cummin and gooin cos of his clogs, tha con heear 'em in t' next street but ah've never eeard him all week."

"Appen he's weearin shoes," sed Ada.

"Never! he's worn clogs fer years, they're his trade mark as yo might say."

Ah couldn't picture Tom wi' shoes on.

"He might not want thi to see him," ses Ada in a funny sort of a way.

"Appen he's got company."

"Nay, not owd Tom," ah wer fair flummoxed, "ah've never known him say owt bar pass the time o' day. You dooan't think as he's picked up wi' somebody do you?"

"Ah'm saying nowt no more," decided Ada but she knew mooar nor she wer letting on.

There wer no clogs gooin past mi dooar fer weeks and ah missed 'em. It wer just like loysing summat.

Then as ah wer swilling t' flags one Saturday morning who cums past but Tom, new suit, new cap and new shoes. Ada wer reet then.

Ah didn't know whether to speyk, he luked that different, a bit uncomfortable, sheepish if yo will.

"Mornin Tom."

He just nodded and went on deawn t' street, he didn't seem to walk reight to me, not wi' shoes on.

"Yo must a' bin reight," ah towd Ada later on when ah towd her as ah'd seen Tom gooin eawt all dressed up. He'd ne'er get all rigged up like yon to go eawt on his ooan.

Ada sed nowt, just smiled as if she knew summat as ah didn't.

A neet or two afther that ah wer listening to mi wireless and ah cud a' sworn as ah heeard Tom's clogs gooing past. That wer a surprise but just to be sure as ah weren't heearing things ah left mi dooar oppen a bit and reight on time ah heeard him shout, "good neet," and somehow ah wer reight suited.

Ah geet the full story from Ada next day when ah towd her as t' clogs wer back. It seems he'd copped on wi' a widda deawn at t' pub.

This widda wer fed up o' being on her ooan and Tom wer a nice enough chap. It had gone awreet at first. He'd even geet shoes to please her and fotched her whooam fer a bit o' supper, seems like he wer fair tekken on wi her as weel.

They hed very nearly got reawnd to naming t' day when she med her mistake.

She towd Tom as she'd tidy t' place up a bit when she cum to live theer and he sed it'd be awreet as long as she left things as he wer used to. He needed new curtains and a new carpet and that wer awreet, he reckoned as he'd be hevvin more company once he wer wed so he didn't mind spending a bit to brighten t' place up.

Then he geet a sickener, she sed as neaw he'd started weearing shoes he'd hev to get rid of his clogs. She sed as if they wer hevvin a new carpet she weren't hevvin it ruined wi' him walking allo'er it wi' clogs on.

"Nay, 'owd on," ses Tom "this is my heawse and if ah get a new carpet ah'll walk on it wi' mi clogs on". Shoes wer awreet when tha wer cooarting but he'd rayther hev his clogs and they wer better fer thi feet speshully in t' bad weather.

Then t' widda sed as none of her friends wore clogs any more as they wer owd fashioned.

"Weel" ses Tom, "ah'm nooan getting rid o' my clogs so tha con tek it or leave it."

She must a' left it cos as ah sed he hed his clogs back on and ah saw a van fotching a carpet to his dooar.

Ah never saw his lady friend although ah live next dooar but he seems awreet bowt her.

It meks a nice ending to t' day when ah heear them clogs and Tom shouts "Good Neet" as he goes whooam on his ooan.

It is strange how certain Lancashire towns have become associated with clogs. There's Colne, the home of Colne irons (extra thick, heavy-duty tackle). Pendlebury folk are known as "Purrers, which is a dialect word for "puncing" or kicking - handed down from the time of clog-fighting, that most barbaric of sports. Associated with the same aspect of the clog's use is the Darwen Billy, a sharp-pointed, brass-bound clog. It is recalled that a football match took place in 1830 between Tottington and Darwen at Turton. The Press reporter recorded "*....they had turned out in proud array, each man wearing a clean shirt, white stocking, a boot on one foot to kick the ball and a Darwen Billy clog on the other to kick his opponents.*"

Speaking of sayings connected with clogs ....*"Ah'm thad 'ungry, Ah could eyt a buttered clog"* .... *"Hoo's getten a face tha could clog"* (She has a rather leathery complexion) ...*"From clogs to clogs in three generations"* I record a few more in "Concerning Clogs".

Speaking too of clog-fighting, let's hear of a Lancashire equivalent of the *"Gunfight at OK Corral"*. This saga was written by Alan and Les Bond, who both wore clogs as lads. I know that for certain. They climbed t' coits and played football with me in mi grandma's back, and med sparks in St John's yard. You'll love this:-

THE CLOG FEYTER

In a town just east of Blackburn
near the Church and Ossie border
in Accrington lived Cloggie Joe,
a mon of sheer dis-order.

He were t' worlds clog-feytin champion
and knew all t' clogs feyters tricks
from lashin out wi booath feet
to sneaky back foot flicks.

He's beat the best for miles around
held the Golden Clogs Award,
he fought for t' North Lancs Tripe Dressers
and always swept the board.

But Joe were a dirty feyter
an' he liked to set the pace,
he'd chew on lumps of garlic
which made him hard to face.

From breathed out clouds of acrid fumes
opponents fell away
advantage Joe...he'd come in low
an' punce em where they lay.

Now Joe got reyt conceited
an' he strutted down the street
with his new lead weighted training clogs
(to give him stronger feet).

He staggered in T' Duck an' Trumpet
where t' landlord cross-eyed Mick
stirred his beer up wi clog irons
(to give it extra kick).

Joe's girlfriend were sat there in t' corner
stutterin Bertha Magee,
she'd a figure like t' lamplighters donkey
an' a face like a busted settee.

Hoe geet her a pint o' lampoil shandy
and needin summat stronger to face her
said "Gimme a pint o' best bitter
wi' half a pint Iron Brew chaser".

He were takin drinks o'er to Bertha
when a stranger come clatterin in
wearin' the biggest pit boots
that Joe or his cronies 'ad sin.

A gasp came from owd 'arry Pickersgill
like a rapid deflatin car tyre
cos he knew who it were, an he knew why he'd come
an he knew then that fat were in fire.

T' stranger looked at Joe's clogs wi a smirk on 'is face
looked Joe up an down wi' a sneer,
yo could hear a pin drop when he said wi' a growl
"Tha fancies thi sel so I hear."

Up from his seat jumped 'owd 'arry
and spoke up so all t' pub could hear,
"It's Pit Boot Punce Champion fra Wigan
an' he won t' Lonsdale Boot just last year."

"You're challenging me?" said Joe wi a laugh,
"I've come for thi crown" said the lad,
an cross eyed Mick said "If th'art challenging Joe
tha's got to be barmy or mad".

They kicked off outside t' Duck an Trumpet
puncin' each other around
from one side o' t' town to the other
but nayther o' t' feyters went down.

They fought until long after sunset
till both were exhausted and raw,
an each knew he couldn't lick t' other
so at last they agreed on a draw.

Later in t' thowd Duck an Trumpet
they both were the toast of the town
they stood with their arms round each other,
as pint after pint they put down.

They were so full of bloated importance
as they told of each others careers
they didn't hear Daisy's "Excuse me",
her request to pass fell on deaf ears.

"Excuse me", she said a bit louder
"I want to get through to the bar,"
but both Bob and Joe decided
they weren't going to move very far.

They say she moved faster than lightening
as she lifted her skirt to her knees
and a double-legged, roundhouse backslider
felled both Bob and Joe like two trees.

Daisy stepped over both fallen heroes
and ordered a drink at long last
then, without batting an eyelid she said
"tha' should get out o' t' way when tha'rt asked.

What happened to em after's a mystery
for neither was heard of again
some say that they both emigrated
and some say they both died of shame.

So remember if you are a fighter
with fist or with boot or with clog
it isn't the size of the dog in the fight
it's the size of the fight in the dog.

Fred Mills won 2nd prize in the dialect writing competition organised by the Lancashire Authors Association in 1969 with the following story. I have been unable to trace him to ask his permission to print this, but I don't want to leave it out because it is so good and so I take the liberty of using his work without formal permission:-

A PAIR O' LANKYSHEER CLOGS

When eawr little Alice Ann wur abeawt twelve months owd, mi mother sez to me: "Hey, that lass is noan shappin' for walkin' yet. You'll ha' to try my mother's recipe, as hoo used wi' eawr lot. You mun get that chilt a pair o' clogs. Hoo'll be on her feet in no time, or Aw'm sadly chetted. Tek her to owd Alfert to be measured. He'll mek a gradely job on it."

Aye, he wur a rare mon at his job, wur owd Alfert. Noan o' these here machine-made clog-soles for him. Naw, th' owd lad could cut eawt a pair o' wooden soles just to t' shape o' your feet. If you'd anny bunions, corns, hommer-toes or owt, he'd skive t' leather an' hollow t' sole till it felt reet.

Dun you remember, folk in eawr younger days thowt there wur nowt like clogs for foot comfort. They'd put their shoon on at Sundays to goo to t' church or t' chapel. As soon as they geet whoam off ud come them shoon, an' th' owd clogs ud goo an agen. It wur t' same when they went on their holidays. Aye, an' lots on 'em took their clogs to Blackpool wi' 'em to res their feet. One mon as Aw knew, he couldn't afford t' railway fare; so he walked o t' road fro' Burnley to Blackpool wearin' his clogs. He carried his shoon wi' him an' put em on when he geet theer.

Aw took eawr little lass to be measured for her fust pair o' clogs. Owd Alfert howded her tiny feet in his wark-worn honds as if he wur blessin' 'em. "Ai, what bonny little toes-toes," he sez. "Aw wonder wheer these little tootsies ull tek thi afore that dees. T' other end o' t' world, happen." (Th' owd lad ne'er knew what a true prophet he wur. By gum, hoo's in New Zealand wi' her family neaw).

Gooin' in owd Alfert's shop browt back mem'ries o' mi own schoo'-days. We o on us wore clogs then, well, nobbut one or two as thowt they wur summat. Mony a neet afther t' schoo' there'd be abeawt hawf-a-dozen of us lads sittin' on Alfert's form - he wurn't owd Alfert then - waitin' to have eawr clogs mended. Happen it ud be a freysh set o' eyorns, a cappel, or a tin plate on t' toe. (We wur awlus breykin' eawr clog-noses in wi' puncin' stones or tin cans.) Sometimes t' sole itsel' wur brokken. Then it wur a job o' seein' if they'd 'clog' agen. That's heaw th' owd Lankysheer sayin' started. If a widow wur lookin' for a freysh felly; "Hoo'd like to clog agen".

Winter-time wur hard on lads' clogs. We used to goo skeytin' on t' frozzen lodges, an' that soon wore th' eyorns eawt. Us lads had another trick. We'd kick sparks off t' kerb-stones; an' that didn't mend things.

Clogs were used for feytin' an' o. They do reckon as when they box in France they use their feet an' co' it "savate". We co'ed it "purrin" 'em. But if you "purred" a lad when he wur deawn, that wurn't clen feytin'. Aw've seen mony a lass tek her clog off an' pummel a lad wi' it. If he run away hoo'd say: "If Aw corn't catch thi my dog con", an' throw her clog afther him. Them wur roof days.

Neaw you'll hardly e'er see a pair o' clogs, nobbut if a mon works deawn t' pit, in wather, or summat like that. (Oh aye, an' you met sometime see t' Morris-Dancers at a carnival, we' bells on their fancy clogs.)

To get back to owd Alfert; while he wur measurin' t' chilt's feet, Aw axed him heaw things wur shappin' in his trade. He sez; "Ai, t' cloggin's welly played eawt. A toothri chaps wears 'em. But t' days o' clogs (an' shawls) for women, it's gone an' forgetten. Women put their feet in thin, fancy shoes wi' papper soles an' peg-top heels. They wobble abeawt like ducks in leggin's, an' get their feet wichert every time it rains. But thee tek it fro' me, there's still nowt like a gradely pair o' clogs to keep you feet o reet in a Lankysheer winter".

Well, when them Size 1 clogs wur finished they wur a seet for sore een. They'd brass nails o reawnd an' fancy little clasps.

Me and Mary, we marched reawnd to grandma's wi t' clogs an' eawr Alice Ann. Mi mother, hoo stroked them clogs an' looked at 'em as if they wur Cinderella's gowden slippers. "Ai, them's summat like. Neaw, let's have 'em on, an' put her on that theer table."

Grandma howded t' child under th' armpits, wi' clogs just touching t' white-wood table. Eawr little lass danced an' stamped an' crowded to yer what a noise hoo could mek on that table-top. By gum, but it worked o reet. In less nor a week that chilt wur agate a-walkin'. Aye, an' when eawr Nancy coom, them clogs coom in agen for t' same job.

When eawr Alice Ann grew up hoo claimed them little clogs an' kept 'em for a keepsake. Aye, an' when hoo geet wed hoo took 'em we' her to New Zealand; an' at t' other side o' t' world there's four moor little childer what's larn to walk wi' them little clogs. Aw'll bet them kiwis han fairly gawped at 'em.

Ai, an' let me tell you summat. Alice Ann towd me in her last letter as there'd bin a competition on their T.V. t' other week. It wur for t' most unusual souvenir as annybody could show. What dun you think won it? Why, that little pair o' Lankysheer clogs.

A different slant on the clogs theme has been found by Tom Haworth. Like all good clog stories, there's a kick in the last line:-

SHINY CLOGS

Ther wor a lad in eawr schoo',
Who never geet sums reet;
Bud in wun thing 'e really shone -
'Is clogs wur shiny breet.

Us other lads aw laughed at 'im,
Puncin' a ball abeawt;
While 'e sat a' whoam each neet
Wi' blackin' brush an' cleawt.

When it wor time t' find a job,
An' times wor really 'ard,
Whey wor eawtside, but 'Shiny Clogs'
Wor walkin' deawn t' mill yard.

Then come th' age t' start coortin' -
Aw fancied Jane, reet bad,
But lookin' at mi scruffy clogs
Hoo smiled an' sed, 'Nay, lad.'

Hoo went an' wedded 'Shiny Clogs':
Neaw they've three chilther fine,
If Aw'd a bin a bit moor preawd,
Yon chilter might bi mine.

Neaw Aw'm just sittin' on mi own,
Wi t' cat an' t' china dogs:
If Aw'd mi time all o'er agin
Aw wouldn't ayf shine mi clogs.

Aw'll bet when St. Peter siz 'im,
'E'll say: 'Ne'er mind thi sin -
Ah like the look of thi clogs, mate,
Thart welcome, come reet in."

My friend Mary Smith has captured, in just a few lines, the story of clogs and Lancashire. This should be made compulsory reading in Lancashire schools (even though the second line contains a historical inaccuracy - it is highly likely that clogs were in use in England long before the Flemish weavers came over to Bolton. See the fuller explanation in "Concerning Clogs")

CLOGS

It's several hundred year sen clogs cum to Lancashire.
They copped on fost in Bowton, afooer they landed here.
There's various different sooarts o' clogs to suit the job you do,
Strung pit clogs, worn bi colliers to stop t' pick gooin' through.
Duck bills were known as cooartin' clogs, booath tops an' soyls were leet,
Sooa as they cud walk past verra quaat, when out wi' lass at neet.
Dancin' clogs were thin an' leet an' curved frae heel to toe,
Wi patterned tops an' fancy tabs, breet nails to fairly glow.
Nah t' later ones hed clasps or straps, an' some laced reet to t' top,
Sooa yo' never dud get witchert, an' cowds yo' dudn't cop.
To cleyn eawr clogs we hed to use Bury blackin' in a stick
An' shave it off, an' mix it up wi' watter till it went thick.

We hed no brush to spreyd it on: we used a rappet's foot,
An' when we'd done we weshed it out an' hung it on a hook.
We then left clogs till they geet dry; next mornin' they'd be reet
For t' velvet pad an' elbow grease - by gum, it med'em breet!
When Ah were young, to keep me in they med me wear mi clogs,
But sometime durin' t' day Ah'd squat mi shoon round t' prata hogs:
At neet Ah'd out an' put 'em on, then off to meet mi lad
But Ah hed to mind as Ah geet back in th' house afooer mi dad!
There is nowt better fer yer feet than clogs, if they're weel med,
An' they cum in lots o' colours now, frae black to fiery red.
But sum sooart don't hev irons on, sooa they wain't met a spark -
We used t' hev fun, when Ah were young, out sparkin' after dark.
A pair o' clogs are priceless when put on t' babby's feet:
That child will walk wi' confidence, an' they'll keep its ankles reet.
An' if fowk allus weear clogs, they'll never hev bow-legs
Or be like Ike, as hed a corn, an' tooas covered wi' segs.
In summer, clogs help keep you cool, yo'll ne'er hev sweaty feet,
Like some as weear shoon aw day an' stink yo' out at neet.
An' weear yer clogs when out at neet, then a mugger yo con defy;
Punch him weel on booath shins - let him taste o' clog toe pie.
An' sooa, don't let tradition die, wi' pride now let us weear
Eawr clogs, sooa aw the world may know we come frae Lancashire.

I have mentioned the nickname "Purrers" being given to Pendlebury folk. They're quite proud of it, as is evidenced in the following lines by Emily Arden:-

CLOGS (by a Pendlebury Purrer)

If tha wants fer t' talk abairt clogs, tha's cum t' t' reet shop. When Ah were a little lass Ah allas used t' wurr 'em both fer gooin 't t' schoo', an' fer playin' airt in t' street. Th' oney time Ah used t' wurr shooes were fer gooin' t' Sunday Schoo' an' t' Chapel. Ah remember weel t' clogs as Ah 'ad were them as fastened wi' a clasp across t' front o' t' foot, but one time sum o' mi mates gor agate a-wurrin' wot were cawed "slipper-clogs". Them were t' soart wi' a strap across th' ankle an' a round shiny button as fastened at t' side. Well, nowt ud do but Ah 'ad t' have a purr o' them. Ah fair meithered me Mam's brains airt till Ah geet sum. Well, as tha'll know to thi cost, it were 'ell's own job gerrin' used to new clogs; wot wi' sore 'eels an' bleedin' ankles - ee! by gow! Ah suffered summat shockin', Ah can tell thi', but Ah mastered 'em at t' finish, an' Ah geet some good wurr airt on 'em.

Best were when t' snow were on t' grainnd, walkin' abairt in it, gerrin' it aw stuck in between t' clog-irons, till it were aw piled up i' great big pads under thi feet. Ee! tha used t' feel ten foot tall.

Another pastime used t' be runnin' up an' dairn t' street i't' dark of a Winter's neet, bangin' thi clog-irons o' t' flags an' makin' t' sparks fly, seein' oo could make t' best show.

One game we used t' enjoy were collectin' bits o' brocken clog-irons, an' wi' used t' tek it i' turns fer t' chuck 'andful up i' thi' air, an' t' one as catched mooist were t' winner.

But best of aw were gooin' t' t' cloggers fer t' get thi clogs fettled. T' shop weer wi' used t' goo 'ad bin a cake-shop at one time, an' it 'ad shelves reet up t' t' ceilin', an' while wi' waited fer air clogs bein' done, wi used fer t' be climbin' all ower t' shelves like a cartload o' monkeys. Ah used fer t' like watchin' t' clogger purrin' little bits o' matchsticks i' th' holes weer t' nails 'ad bin, then placin' new iron on, an' 'ammerin' t' little nails in. 'E used t' have a bucket o' summat as 'e dipped t' new clog-irons in afore 'e put 'em on. 'E used t' call it "Owd Lant" bur Ah fun airt after, as it were "wee-wee". No wonder t' place 'ad a rum soart o' smell abairt it! 'E were as bald as a badger, were t' clogger, an' no wonder when Ah think wor 'e pur up wi', wi' us childer.

Sad part abair it were, aw this fun come to a suddin' stop when Ah went an' geet a Scholarship to t' Grammar Schoo', an' 'ad fer t' start a wurrin' shooes an' talkin' proper.

Margaret Greenhalgh, a sadly-missed lover of Lancashire and its folk, mourns the passing of clogs in her poem:-

CLOGS

Ya durn'd si monny clogs abaht
Sin' shoes 'ev t'en ther places,
Wi' bits o' shiny tin o' t' toes,
Er teed wi' leather laces.
Bud when folk weren'd so gradely off -
It's o' th' owd days Ah'm talkin' -
A' t' babbies 'ed a pair o' clogs
To ged 'em used to walkin'.

When t' childer traycled off to t' schoo'
To ged ther bit o' larnin,
Ya'd 'ear 'em rattle rahnd t' schoo' yard
At nine o'clock i' t' mornin'.
A't' bonny weyvers wore 'em then,
An' t' bits o' lasses tentin' -
Thi med 'em shine like lukkin'-glass
Wi' tuthree bits o' fentin'.

Then t' knocker-up, 'e wore 'em, too,
An' 'is were noisy tackle,
'E 'ed a' t' folk theer wakkened up

Afoor thi 'eeard 'is rattle.
Ya'd 'ear 'em clatterin' up an dahn,
Wi' t' postman an' wi' th' 'awkers,
An' t' little lads o' t' flags i' t' street,
A' mekkin' sparks wi' t' cokers.

Ya'd 'ev a job to ged 'em nah,
Ah durn'd know wheer ya'd buy 'em -
Fer folk 'ev getten' snooty-like,
An' too stuck-up to try 'em.
Thi traipse arahnd i' platform shoes,
Aye, t' lads as weel as t' lasses,
Wi's never si th' owd clogs ageean -
Thi've gone wi' th' owd 'oss brasses.

I've been unable to trace Walter F. Hampson, who won 2nd prize in the 1948 Lancashire Authors Association dialect writing competition, but take the liberty of showing it off here as I believe it ought to be read by a wider public.

THOOSE LITTLE CLOGS

Eh dear o' me these littel clogs,
Whatever mun Aw do?
They're lyin theer slutched up to t' top,
An' soaked wi wayter too.

There's one o' th toes punced welly in,
An' one o' th soles is split;
An' t' little irons are var near done,
They're worn aboon a bit.

An' t' mon as wears 'em he's a limb,
He's t' roughest lad i' th street;
He goes a feeshin' deawn i' th bruck,
An' gets his stockins weet.

He comes whum daubed reet up to th' een,
Wi clay, an' paint an' tar;
An' brings his frogs an' tiddlers, in
A nasty pickle jar.

He comes whum limpin' monny a time,
Wi' greight black marks an' cuts;
He comes in monny a time a day,
For cake an' trackle buts.

Aw know eaur Bill's a little rogue,
Sometimes he's gradely nowt;
He rips his clooas an' breiks his clogs
A rollockin' yung cowt.

Aw've chunnert an' Aw've saused him weel,
Aw've fot him monny a clout;
Aw met as weel just save mi wind,
T' yung beggar cares for nowt.

To see him when he's fast asleep,
He looks as good as gowd;
Yo' wouldn't think 'at he could be
So troublesome an' bowd.

An' when Aw goes to tuck him up,
An' mak' him snug i' bed,
Aw connot help but lay mi hond
Upon his curly yed.

Maybe Aw shouldn't fratch so much,
Lads will bi lads they sen,
Aw'll not begrudge him his bit o' fun -
A marlock neaw an' then.

Aw like yon little pair o' clogs,
An' t' mon as wears 'em too,
Aw like to yer 'em rattle, when
He's comin' whum fro t' skoo.

Eh bless his bonny breet blue een,
An' bless his curly yed;
Aw'll tak' another look at him,
Afore Aw goo to bed.

In 1973, I spoke to my mate Jack Benson and asked if he had written anything on a clogs theme for my collection. He hadn't, but within a few days there arrived through my letter box:-

CLOGS

I see a pair o' clogs an' straight away I start to think
O' fowk I've known, or happen wish I hed,
For clogs, to me, sum up a deal o' people as I've met,
Some livin' yet an' some a fair while dead.

They're solid an' dependable,
They'll seldom let thee down.
They've character an' habits o' their own.
They'll waarm thee when tha needs it most,
An' down some lonely street
They'll cheer thee, clatt'rin, when tha'r most alone.

A pair o' bran new clogs, hast' e'er sin owt as sweet i' life?
Th'owd cloggers hard-earned cunnin's sarved him weel.
Black leather wi' brass lacehoils, aye an' leather tha con smell,
Aw standin' firm atop o' cokered steel.

When we were lads o' frosty days,
Ee how we used to slide
An' pick up snow pads, six foot high tha'd be,
They reckon as tha seldom sees a clog these days i' town,
But here i' th' country clogs'll never dee.

So here's to clogs at wark i' th' oppen fields fra morn till neet,
Or out i' th' shippon yard some cowd forenoon.
An' slutchy clogs as wait o' th' step while th' owd mon eyts his tae,
I'll lift me glass to clogs, to gradely shoon.

There are very few poems that can be dated with any degree of accuracy, but I can positively state that the next poem was written a few days before 25th October 1980, which is the date on which I received a 'phone call from lovely Louisa Bearman at Bolton. She 'phoned to give me permission to use one of her poems in my book, and casually mentioned that she had just composed another poem. Did I want to hear it? Louisa hadn't written it down as she is blind, but she'd be glad if I would write it. It didn't have a title, so I've called it:-

BRASS CONSCIOUS

When Ah wer young, wi wer cawd "th' upper working class".
Mi dad wer t' foreman up at t' mill.
An' o' course, he geet more brass.
Ah'd a special frock fer Sunday,
An' breawn shoes fer that day,
An' used fer t' swank it up a bit
O'er t' poor uns deawn the way.
Ah'd bin t' Sunday Schoo one wik end,
An' when Ah geet awum,
A chap were exin dad fer wark,
An' he'd browt his little son.
Eh lass, mi feyther sed to me,
Tek t' laddie fer a walk.

Tek him eawt an' show him t' fleawrs
So his dad an' me can talk.
"No", Ah sed, "He's clogs on,
An' it's Sundi afternoon"
So mi dad put my clogs on,
An' took away mi shoon.
"Theer", he said, "Thar't booath alike,
An' just tek heed, mi lass.
Thar't nobbut one bit better
Because we've geet mooar brass".

Dear Doris Hodgson living in St Michael's village had a countrywoman's common-sense view of the qualities of clogs and the worth (?) of fashionable footwear:-

WIMMIN'S SHOON

Wen I wer a nipper we aw wore clogs
Wi cokers wat sumtimes ud spark,
As wi ran ower th' cobbles i' time ta get o'am
Afore we were lokt out i th' dark.
Thi wer gradely an' warm tho' fer playin' i th' slush
An' fer keeping wer' feet dry i th' snow,
Witch stuk ta wer cokers i' such greyt big lumps
Wat wer ard as an' owd cricket baw.

A few years later th' owd clogs wer put by
Fer shoon wat wer different i' style,
Wi tooes wat were long as an owd weesel's snout
An eels wat stuck up aif a mile
Thi just looked like h'ostriches struttin' alon'
But ah bet aw their tummies went round,
If thi cum ta sum spots wot ud just catch ther eels.
An' bring um aw tumblin' ta th' ground.

But things wot yung wimmin is weering ta day
Thi don't aif luk ugly, gor lummy,
Thi luk like th' owd boxes wot th' Eegipshun kings
Used ta use wen thi stored up ther mummy.
Next year thi'll hav disks in fer top o' t' pops
Er th' stuff wot thi put on ther mugs,
An aw wi owd codgers u'll heo ta fork out
Fer ear plugs ta stuff i wer lugs.

Nora Howorth's father had similar views, clearly born of the experience of years:-

CLOGS

Mi Father, when retirement came,
Was gardening all day long,
As happy as a sandboy,
Till things started going wrong.
His shoes got scratched and muddy,
His feet got sopping wet -
And Mother [always finicky]
Began to get upset.
She said 'You'll catch your death o' cowd,
As well as spoil your shoes -
And we don't want your funeral, mind,
As front page local news.
So let's postpone that sad event;
You need some rubber boots!'
But Father said, 'Howd on, theer, lass,
I think you'll find it suits
Mi purposes best to get some clogs
To keep me warm and dry'.
'To get some clogs! Whatever next?'
Said Mother with a sigh.

'You can't wear clogs on this estate,
What would the neighbours say?'
She questioned somewhat snobbishly,
But Father had his way.
He got the car, and started up,
And drove to Garstang town,
Wi Mother muttering 'Wearing clogs!
He'll really let us down'.
Dad marched across them cobblestones
In t' front o' t' Royal Oak,
And Mother trailed behind him.
But not a word she spoke,
As into t' little shop went Dad,
Dressed in his Sunday togs,
And stood and stated firmly;
'Ah want a pair o' clogs.
That's what ah said, it's clogs I need,
To keep me warm and dry'.
'He want some clogs, and that's a fact',
Said Mother with a sigh.

An' found him just t' right size,
So t' fellows there, they showed him some,
While Mother looked around her

And could scarce believe her eyes.
Some brightly coloured little clogs
Were on a shelf near t' door -
They made her think o' t' childer -
She's Grandma now to four.
Remembering childhood's clog-clad days
And all the fun she'd had;
Or later on when in her teens
And courtin' wi' mi' Dad,
She looked again. They looked so cute
In green, red, white, or blue.
She whispered 'I'll buy some o' them
When they're through serving you
Y' know, fer t' childer - just the job!
They're such a bonny style.
I want some clogs - let's all have clogs!'
Said Mother with a smile.

Still on the qualities of clogs, I quote Dr. Hindle, a School Medical Officer at Haslingden many years ago:- "*The clothing and footgear of the children were of a very satisfactory nature. The children as a whole are well fed and sensibly dressed, clogs being the usual footgear worn by them. ...A good pair of clogs is in my opinion, as serviceable as a good pair of boots. I would much sooner that a child of mine wore a good pair of clogs than a poor pair of boots ....Have you ever noticed that many walking performances in which men set out to do a certain mileage in a certain time are done by men who wear clogs at the time?*"

Brian Clare, a master of the art of touching the heart-strings, was the first winner of the "Samuel Laycock Trophy" and the Lancashire Dialect Society's certificate at the Fylde Folk Festival, Fleetwood 1979 with this poem:-

RECOLLECTIONS

Sittin up on't top ut moor
Back ugen uh sun-warm'd waugh,
Lookin daewn threw't th' haze tu wom
Time stands still us a recaw.

Pipe weel lit, a seyk un puff
Mi idle fingers tap mi clug,
Memories flood back tu mi mind
Us a stroke un scrat mi little dug.

Her sits un looks wi yed cock't oer,
Her knows am deep i thowt.
Sittin, waitin patiently,
Wi nar u move ner nowt.

Gooin't scoo comes tu mi mind
Clutchin mi mammy's hond,
Neys uh clugs on't th'owd flagged yard,
Fot memories frum beyond.

Wid happy times ut walkin days
Brass Bands play'd unt th' horses prance't
Cheery, clatterin seynds ut clugs
Us foak spun, un wheel't, un skip't un dance't.

Sadness too, thoose clugs fot back
Frum t' days when't strike wer ut its hey't
Hungry childer, skrikin wimmen
Short temper't men, beaut wark, beaut meight.

Ney, if yo ask't mit give uh sign
Hey't tell Lanky foak yu meet
It ud be tu look fert clugs
They wore upon ther feet.

Fer clugs ah know, uv spanned ma life.
Frum t' child't-int-th' arms tut present day
Av nar bin beaut ah pair, ah never will!!
Until ah dee un deep in graewnd ah lay.

Common wer clugs i times gone by
Yu cud harken um neet un day
Worn bi every soart uh foak
Boath fer ther wark un fer ther play.

Its not oft yu con hear um naew
Thi seeum t' be in't past
But in mi mind, safe locked uway
Ther memory'll allus last.

Fer clugs, like caps, un scarves, un brats
Are allus welcome here
Fert seynd uh clugs meuns wum to me
Un wum meuns Lancashire!!!

Fancy a pint? Why not try one at *"The Boot and Clogger"*, Hyde Road, Woodhey, Stockport (it's built on the site of an old clog shop), or *"The Clogger's Arms"*, Uppermill, Oldham, or *"The Clogger's Arms"*, Oldham Road, Failsworth. (This is known locally as *"Top Clogger's"* because there used to be a *"Bottom Clogger's"* too), or *"The Clog and Billycock"* at Blackburn, so called because a one-time landlord wore those items of apparel, as did the timber-trade workers who frequented the old pub, formerly called *"The Bay Horse"*.

Schooldays in Oldham are recalled by Edith Ralphs, (note her use of the phrase "slippy curry"):-

CLOGS

Willie Smith wer' owt' but pleased
In fact he looked quite glum
Thur' wer' summut' ut' he wanted
Un' he'd ave to ax' his Mum.

He shivered as he glanced abeawt
Fer' t' greawnd wer' frozzen ard'
His pals wer' avin' lots o' fun
As thi' ran abeawt School Yard.

But he, like "Greta Garbo"
Ad' to bi' alone
He felt fed up un' dejected
Like o' dog witheawt o' bone.

Bill wore shoes wi' rubber soles
So heaw could he feel merry
His feet debarred him of a game
Wit' lads on t' "Slippy Curry".

"Rubber scrotches th' ice," a young friend sed'
"Just go un' ax' mi' brother"
"Un' anyway play bi' yerself"
"You go un' mak' another".

Young William felt his happiness
Ad' flown un' gone to t' dogs
So after School he sed "Please Father
Con I ave' some clogs"?

His Mother sed, E'h Albert
He con' ave' o' pair surely
If he keeps worritin' like this
Wer' beawnt to ave' him poorly".

"O' reet then, let him ave' some clogs"
Sed Father, "but by heck
I hope yuv' got him well insured
Cause he'll break his bloomin neck".

"Thanks Mum, thanks Dad," sed Willie
"But Oh! please could yu' hurry?
Because if o' thaw set in yu' see
Ther' won't bi' a "slippy curry".

One group who still wear clogs are farmers. David Lavisher tells of one farmer and his clogs:-

OWD FARMER ENTHWISTLE'S CLOGS

Thi wer sellin up farmhouse and t' buildings.
Everythin', exeptin' t' dogs.
Ah decided ta tek stock o' t' tack-room,
Ther wern't a reet lot left ta log.
A currycomb, 'orse-shoes, an buckles,
An owd Farmer Enthwistle's clogs.

Thi'd born up well, wi' t' standin,
Mildewed, but still fairly good.
One an 'alf laces still threaded,
An th' irons wer still nailed ta t' wood.
A reet sturdy piece a work thi wer.
Thi'd served th' owd farmer reet well.
An as Ah think back, some thirty odd years,
There's a little owd tale a can tell.

'E'd bin out fer a drink, after t' milkin'.
It wer dark, wen e'd getten w'om.
'E'd took off 'is clogs, 'e kept trippin'.
'E'd absorbed a gallon, then some.
A'll sneak clogs upstairs, wer 'is thinkin'.
So 'e tucked 'em up under 'is jacket.
'E stood on t' cat, as wer lyin' at top,
An thi a' tumbled down, wat a racket.
'Is missus appeared up on t' landin',
"Ger out a mi 'ouse, wi yer clogs".
Shi threw 'im an t' clogs intat farmyard,
An fer good measure, booted out t' dogs.

E'd give dogs a clog each ta carry,
'We'll sleep in th' owd tack-room', 'e said,
One at dogs died, it wer poisoned,
An t' other went out uv its 'ead.
'E woke up at five, followin' morning,
'E'd not slept a wink a' neet.
'E'd used one at clogs as a pilla,
It ponged; aye, 'is missus wer reet.

'E left pair a clogs in th' owd tack-room,
'Cos Wellington Boots 'e'd bi gettin',
'E could stand in a puddle an' wash 'em,
An walk reet in th'ouse wi'out frettin'.

A'll pinch these clogs from th'owd tack-room.
Still covered in what makes grass grow.
There's a reet lot more stories surround 'em,
A'll tell 'em thi sometime, ya know.

Stella Blainey thinks that nothing changes in this world, and that there's nothing new. The clogs of yesteryear are the "fashion clogs" of today:-

HEIGHT O' FASHUN

Ah 'member mi mam in 'er clogs an' 'er shooerl,
As shi set eawt fer t' mill uvva mooarnin,
An' t' noise o' t' clogs on th'owd cobblt rooad
Fur rung eawt as each week-day wur dooarning'.

Well, mi wife, Mary Ann, warkt int' mill like t' rest
But thi warn't weearin' clogs then sa mooch like.
Still, shi kep' wun ont' shelf, wot shi wooer as a child
To show t' kids 'ow thur muther wooer such like.

Neaw mi dooarter, Louise- 'er as wuks on t' looms-
Wudda turn't oop 'er noeas at such weearin'.
Shi weears treawsers like me an' a black leather cooat
As is mooar like a man's, Ah'll be sweearin'.

But mi grandooarter, Bess, goos ter't office at t' mill
In wot shi ses is now reet height o' fashun;
Shi calls it a 'ponchoo' [but ter me it's a shooerl],
An' wi' red plastic clogs, shi lukes smashin'!

Let me recommend a booklet to anyone interested in clog-making. It is "*The Clog Maker*", published in 1977 by the Colne Valley Museum, compiled by Howard Bamforth and illustrated by David Norris.

If ever there was anyone who epitomised the Lancashire lass, it was Gracie Fields. Perhaps it was because of her "clogs and shawl" fame that, in 1936 when she launched a boat bearing her name, the Portsmouth and District Lancashire Society presented her with a large bouquet of roses (red, of course) and an ornamental clog.

I've learned that people of different areas have different names for the same thing. This is common knowledge to anyone interested in dialect. There are many dialects within Lancashire, though we usually refer only to "The Lancashire dialect". Bill Carrick wrote to me from Appleby to remind me that in that area the *"pads"* which collect on the bottom of clogs in snow are called *"cogs"* (*"cloggie-boggies"* in other parts) and that what I refer to as *"duck-toed"* clogs (sharp-pointed toes) he has always called *"duck-nebbed"*. They're also called *"duck-bills"*.

I finish on a sad yet hopeful note. I have just looked at a cutting from the *"Sunday Telegraph"* of 5th August 1979. It begins *"Clog-makers are clumping all the way to the bank. Their ancient trade, which once seemed to be on its last legs, is now in the throes of a revival."* It went on to tell of Walkeley's Hebden Bridge Clog Factory having a production boom. Sadly those days are over. The recession affecting industry has hit the firm and they have had to lay off some of the workforce. They are confident however that clogs will win through. You can't keep good men and good products down. The firm are still having parties visiting the factory to watch clogs being made, though many of the visitors prefer to buy gifts made from clogs rather than the clogs themselves.

6. So you want a pair of Clogs?

In an effort to help those people who want a pair of clogs but can't find anywhere to get them, and to help place on record the names of those people who are still making or selling clogs, I have compiled a list. It is as complete and as correct as I can make it but is in no particular order. So far as those listed as "Makers" are concerned, I cannot state whether they make the whole clog in the traditional way or whether they buy ready-made soles and tops then join them together. The customer should enquire first.

MAKERS:
Jack Crawshaw, 56 Miller Barn Lane, Waterfoot, Rossendale.
Clarkson's, (Reuben Truswell) Bridge Street, Garstang. (Tel: 2261)
Walter Hurst, 4 Wigan Road, Hindley, Wigan. (Tel: 55531)
Garside's Footwear, (Jim McNeill) 8 Parrock Street, Crawshawbooth, Rossendale.
R. Turner & Son, 37 Castle Street, Clitheroe. (Tel: 23867)
Rick Rbycki, The Clog Shop, Dale Street, Todmorden. (Tel: 6348)
Jeremy Atkinson, "Kite Clogs", New Lodge Farm, Peterchurch, Herefordshire. (Tel: 377)
Bruce Watson, 203 Hugh Gardens, Newcastle on Tyne.
J.F. Hodgson, 271 Hessle Road, Hull. (Tel: 493849)
Gorphwysfa Instruments, (Trefor Owen) 27 Southfield Lane, Horbury, Wakefield. (Tel: 261260)
Jim Pinnington, Water Street, Todmorden.
Bob Strong, Caldbeck, Cumbria.
Mr Fareo, Ravenglass, Cumbria.
Jack Ashcroft, Chapel Street, Bedford, Leigh.
Lancelot Brew, 54 Roper Street, Whitehaven, Cumbria.
F. Walkley (Clogs) Ltd., Clog Sole Works, Hebden Bridge, Halifax. (Tel: H.B. 2061)
E. Greenwood, 80 Haworth Road, Cross Roads, Keighley.
Pete Sumner, Rose Cottage, 70 Main Road, Long Bennington, Newark, Notts.
R. Butcher, 52 Eldon Street, Preston. (Tel: 56518)
Jim Smith, Mill Street, Coppull, Chorley.
H. Strain, 106 Pall Mall, Chorley. (Tel: 63010)
R. Cropper, 45 Stanifield Lane, Farington, Leyland. (Tel: 22059)
T. Anderton, 6 Hampden-Road, Leyland. (Tel: 22657)

W. Turton, 129 High Street, Skelmersdale.
Alston's Clogs, No 1 Shop, Cattle Market, Brook Street, Preston. (Tel: 718309)
T. K. Matthews, 7 Riley Park, Kirkburton, Huddersfield (Tel: Kirkburton 3102)
George Hogarth, 196 Higher Hillgate, Stockport. (Tel: 061-480-7597)
William Mellor, 17 Yorkshire Street, Bacup.
John Slinger, 32 Coverdale Road, Lancaster. (Tel: 2073)
Mr Marsland, 3 Nursery Street, Sheffield.
Mr Symons, 210 Barnsley Road, Cudworth, S. Yorkshire.
Hywell Davies, Tregaron, Dyfed.
Mike Heseltine, Ffynon Wen Farm, Capel Isaac, Llandeilo, Dyfed. (Tel: Dryslwyn 530)
F. Carroll, 4 High Street, Crewe. (Tel: 212649)
J. Wagstaff, 29 Station Road, Holmfirth, W. Yorkshire.
H.L. Edwards, Derwydd Boot Stores, Conwil Elvert, Dyfed, Carmarthen.

CLOG SELLERS:
Old Father Abraham, 12 Market Street, Hatherleigh, Devon (Tel: 413)
Walco Leather Stores, Head Office, Horne Street, Halifax. (Tel: 58161) Branches:-
Accrington, Ashton-u-Lyne, Barnsley, Birkenhead, Blackburn, Blackpool, Bolton, Bradford, Burnley, Bury, Castleford, Chester, Dewsbury, Doncaster, Eccles, Halifax, Harrogate, Huddersfield, Keighley, Lancaster, Leeds, Leigh, Liverpool, Miles Platting, Nelson, Oldham, Preston, Rawtenstall, Rochdale, Rotherham, St. Helens, Salford, Sheffield, Todmorden, Wakefield, Warrington, Wigan & York. (Many on the telephone)
Briggs Boot Stores, 53 Stricklandgate, Kendal, Cumbria. (Tel: 21335)
Clogs & Wellies, 21 Stricklandgate, Kendal. (Tel: 21335)
Clogs & Wellies, 6 Church Street, Lancaster. (Tel: 34004)
Clogs & Wellies, 30 Main Road, Windermere. (Tel: 5211)
Orpheus Group, The Tricorn, Portsmouth. (Tel: 23044)
Alan Carr, 124 Fleetwood Road North, Thornton-Cleveleys. (Tel: Cleveleys (Tel. 856808)
James Hornby, 123 Station Road, Bamber Bridge, Preston. (Tel: 35831)
Selfit Shoes, Ribbleton Lane, Preston.
N. Memmory & Son, The Market Hall, Blackburn.
E. B. Winn, The Market, Lancaster.
G. Houghton, 16 Higgins Lane, Burscough. (Tel; 892628)
T.R. & E.A. Whittle, Chapel Street, Chorley.

WHOLESALERS IN THE CLOG & LEATHER TRADES:

F. Walkley (Clogs) Ltd., Clog Sole Works, Hebden Bridge. (Tel: 2061)

John Murphy & Son, 1 Clayton Gate, Friargate, Preston. (Tel: 51916)

Thomas Yates, 37 Warner Street, Accrington. (Tel: 34173)

W. Carroll & Son, 4 High Street, Crewe. (Tel: 212649)

Gill & Scholey Ltd., Kingstown Broadway, Carlisle. (Tel: 27624)

Walco Leather Stores Ltd. Horne Street, Halifax. (Tel: 58161)

John T. Scott & Son, Escott Works, Carlisle. (Tel: 24411)

Thomas Green (Silsden) Ltd., Sykes Lane, Silsden, Keighley. (Tel: Steeton 53283)

Walker Last Co.,. Northall Street, Kettering, Northants. (Tel: 4595)

H. Rigby & Son Ltd., Bank Street, Bolton. (Tel: 25134)

McNaught Key & Co., Unit 4, Old Boston Trading Estate, Penny Lane, Haydock, St Helens. (Tel: Garswood Park 712636)

W. Slater & Co. 2 Mill Lane, Blackburn. (Tel: 57928)

Charles Birch & Hipwell, 194 Abbey Hey Lane, Manchester. (Tel: 061 3704263)

E. Howcroft, 180 The Rock, Bury. (Tel: 061 764 4718)

J. Sherratt, 71 Derby Street, Leek, Staffs. (Tel: 382231)

T.P. Walker, 21 Fountain Street, Ulverston. (Tel: 53064)

7. Clogs in Museums

Largely through the perception of museum staff who have forseen that the clogger's art was dying, it is now possible to see reconstructed cloggers' shops in museums at:

Golcar, Huddersfield (Colne Valley Museum) - Tel 659762) Most weekends, visitors can see clogs being made here by the traditional method. On sale here is the excellent booklet "The Clog Maker".

Salford. City Museum, Peel Park. Tel. 061 736 2649. The clogger's shop is just one in a street full of shops of yesteryear. On sale here is Mrs Vigeon's booklet "Clogs, or wooden-soled shoes".

Keighley. (Cliffe Castle Museum) Tel: (0535) 264184

York. Castle Museum (Tel. (0904) 53611. As well as the reconstructed workshop, this Museum also has a collection of glass negatives showing the whole clog-making process, from tree to foot.

Halifax. Shibden Hall Museum. Tel. (0422) 52246

Leeds. Abbey House Museum, Kirkstall. Tel (0532) 755821. This is strictly a cobbler's workshop.

A lot of other Museum Authorities have clogging equipment in their stock, and will be pleased to display it on request.

The Lancashire County Council Museum Service have a stock of clogging equipment and material which they send out to North-West museums periodically. The Chief Museums Officer is John Blundell, Lancashire County Museums Service, Stanley Street, Preston (Tel 56397)

A postcard dated 1916. Perhaps the cards were sold to aid the Edgworth Children's Home.

A trade union certificate of past years. Photo courtesy of the North West Museum Services Unit, Blackburn.